I have no doubt that the po   conflict in our culture today is the abortion   ne tip of the spear where the fiercest spiritual battles are fought is at the entrance to abortion clinics where women make their final life or death decisions regarding their unborn children.

The holy angels of God and the vile demons of hell clash in violent yet unseen spiritual conflict at the entrance to every abortion clinic vying for the life of unborn children and the souls of their parents. The spiritual torment is evident in the strained faces of those who drive onto the property of the abortion clinic intent on terminating a pregnancy. The spiritual angst is seen on the countenance of pro-life sidewalk counselors as they observe each vehicle driving through the gate and later leaving with a broken and weeping woman curled up on the back seat.

Sometimes in life God puts together very unlikely friends. *Connection at the Fence* is the compelling story of just such an unlikely alliance that had to be God-ordained. How else would a dedicated pro-life sidewalk counselor become friends with an abortion clinic employee and not just her but her family? The entire story has the aroma of supernatural connectivity all about it.

You will be captivated by this inside look at the abortion clinic—its employees and clientele. You will begin to appreciate the dedication and passion of sidewalk counselors. You will hear in their own words the heart-breaking stories of women who left a dead child at the abortion clinic, and the exuberant tales of women who turned away at the last moment and are now mothers to precious little children.

Most interesting of all is the dialogue between Shiela and Dionne, two very unlikely friends, as they tentatively begin a relationship—a connection at the fence.

Robert E. Jackson, Jr., M.D.
Author of *The Family Doctor Speaks: The Truth About Life*

Shiela Miller has given us a new slant on pro-life advocacy. Instead of an angry or self-righteous tirade, as a pro-life prayer warrior she stepped out to befriend the workers in her local abortion clinic. The fruit of her kindly outreach is a warm-hearted memoir written with her friend [Dionne Boozer] who still works in the clinic, but who gives an inside story. Reading these personal accounts from both sides of the fence will broaden your insights and build more compassion for all who are caught in the current abortion trap.

Fr. Dwight Longenecker
Pastor of Our Lady of the Rosary Church, Greenville, S.C.
Blogger and Author of *Beheading Hydra –*
A Radical Plan for Christians in an Atheistic Age

Pro-life activist Shiela Miller and pro-choice abortion clinic worker Dionne Boozer have developed a friendship that has led them to realize that they both believe abortion is not the best answer for women who find themselves facing a crisis pregnancy. The life experiences of these two women, who are from opposite sides of the country, will help people on both sides of the abortion issue gain insight into how people may find themselves on opposite sides of the battle. People need to read the book in order to get the details of Boozer's and Miller's stories.

The book is a good read and the details give one a lot of insight into how people find themselves in the situations they are in. *Connection at the Fence* may not have all the answers to how to solve the abortion dilemma, but it is a good starting point to a serious discussion about the need to rethink the approach our nation takes to crisis pregnancies.

Anne Huff
Author of *The Awakening, The Pro-life Movement in South Carolina,*
Learning from the Past to Shape the Future

Dionne Boozer and Shiela Miller are brave women—each one practicing what she believes in—on opposite sides of the abortion clinic perimeter fence. To what degree the conversation each woman has freely engaged in and is chronicled in *Connection at the Fence*, mitigates what course of action she elects to pursue in the days ahead, will only be revealed over time. My hope is that the example of respectful dialogue Dionne and Shiela demonstrate on these pages will shape and inform communities of faith and politics.

John Hoover, Ph. D.
New York Times, Wall Street Journal, BusinessWeek, and
USA Today Bestselling Author

As a member of the medical health professions, I thought I knew about this subject. However, after reading *Connection at the Fence*, I realized there was a lot I didn't know. There is so much humanity involved on both sides of the fence. Everyone wants to do what's best for their situation, but oftentimes are limited in their knowledge. Hopefully, this book will help us all come together and in accordance with Deuteronomy 30:19, "Choose life that you and your seed might live."

Dr. Jack Hancock
Retired Oral Maxillofacial Surgeon
Founding Elder of Mt. Zion Christian Fellowship

Connection at the Fence is one of the most unusual pro-life books I have ever read. It is so interesting and personal that I read it in just a few days. You don't have to agree with everything it says to benefit from it. The story it tells is unfinished but that is the nature of pro-life work and a good reason to be involved, to see what God will do next.

Richard Cash
South Carolina Senator, District 3
Former Pro-life Missionary
Founder, Personhood SC

CONNECTION
at the fence

CONNECTION
at the fence

The Unlikely Friendship Between

An Abortion
Worker

&

A Pro-Life
Advocate

DIONNE BOOZER & SHIELA MILLER

abortion, <u>noun</u>[1]

Definition of *abortion*:

1: the termination of a pregnancy after, accompanied by, resulting in, or closely followed by the death of the embryo or fetus: such as

    a: spontaneous expulsion of a human fetus during the first 12 weeks of gestation – compare MISCARRIAGE

    b: **induced expulsion of a human fetus**

You made all the delicate, inner parts of my body
and knit me together in my mother's womb.

Thank you for making me so wonderfully complex!
Your workmanship is marvelous—how well I know it.

You watched me as I was being formed in utter seclusion,
as I was woven together in the dark of the womb.

You saw me before I was born.
Every day of my life was recorded in your book.
Every moment was laid out before a single day had passed.

Psalms 139:13-16 (NLT)

Dedication

We dedicate this book to saving the unborn, even as we remember
the millions of unborn who are already in God's loving care.

*A five-year-old girl stands outside our abortion clinic
holding her "babies" — two twelve-week fetal models.*

Dedication

To Jean Boozer—thank you for being a living example of a loving mother who sacrifices everything for her children.

Dedication

To Evelyn Honbeck—thank you for choosing life for me and loving me when it was not convenient to be pregnant.[2]

Contents

Foreword   1

Prologue   3

Part One: Introduction to the Fence   5

1 First Encounter with Protestors   6

2 The Conflict of Opposing
Perspectives and Beliefs   10

3 The Pro-Life Movement in Greenville,
South Carolina   15

Part Two: Settling on Opposite
Sides of the Fence   21

4 Dionne's Background   22

5 Shiela's Background   31

Part Three: Working on Opposite
Sides of the Fence   43

6 Working Inside the Abortion Clinic   44

7 Volunteering Outside the Abortion Clinic   68

Part Four: Forming a Connection at the Fence   109

  8 Connecting with Gifts   110

  9 Texting Connection   114

10 Interviewing Dionne   132

Part Five: Conclusions About the Fence   151

11 Reflections   152

12 Final Thoughts   179

Special Thanks   195

Afterword   197

SWITCH   199

Resources   200

Contact the Authors   203

Endnotes   205

Foreword

My name is Dionne, and I've been an abortion worker for 18 years. I never planned to work at an abortion clinic; it just happened. I do believe that a woman has a choice about what happens to her body, but more importantly, I believe that abortion is fundamentally wrong.

Something startling occurred last year: one of the protestors outside the clinic asked me to meet with her after work for a milkshake—we ultimately became friends. And not only did we become friends, but she easily convinced me to chronicle our journey together to help educate others. The plain and simple fact is that women have so many other, better options than terminating a pregnancy through abortion.

My name is Shiela, and three years ago, God called me to be a pro-life advocate outside the abortion clinic in Greenville, S.C. I do not believe in abortion as a viable option for women. I've had the opportunity to speak with hundreds of women while they were driving into and out of the abortion clinic, and I've seen with my own eyes the haunted looks of those who have lost children to abortion. Their stories are very real and very unhappy.

I also believe that pro-lifers can effect a greater change to end abortion if they approach the abortion-minded women and abortion clinic employees with loving, nonjudgmental attitudes.

Employees at the abortion clinic are not generally friendly to the sidewalk counselors, but Dionne was different. I felt the Holy Spirit tug at me to get to know her, befriend her, and eventually, write this book with her. We hope you enjoy reading the story of our journey from fence to friendship.

Prologue

"South Carolinian Shiela Miller waits just outside of [the] private property line. It's 36 degrees, and we're standing outside of the abortion clinic.... She comes here twice a week, rain or shine, for a couple of hours at a time, making sure she has a prayer partner.... [They] do not scream or shout or run in front of cars. Instead, they stand determinedly outside the facility and wave to incoming drivers, praying for an opportunity to share loving, life-affirming alternatives to abortion."

—Kingdomwinds.com[3]

Shiela greets Dionne entering the abortion facility in 2020.

Part One

Introduction to the Fence

1

First Encounters with Protestors

I notice that everyone who supports abortion is alive.
— *President Ronald Reagan*

Shiela writing:

For over a year, I had been coming to stand outside the fence of our local abortion clinic in Greenville, S.C., where babies are routinely terminated during their first trimester of life, six days a week.[4] Two abortionists (referred to in this book as "Dr. One" and "Dr. Two") have taken a staggering combined total of over 100,000 infants' lives since they opened their doors in the 70s.[5] To put that into perspective, nearby Clemson University's Death Valley football stadium only seats 81,500 people.[6]

My pro-life friends and I had formed strong bonds as we created a peaceful and prayerful presence on the public right-of-way beside the driveway into the abortion clinic. I always looked forward to an opportunity to come to the fence to have meaningful conversations with the troubled pregnant girls and women who didn't know all of their options, who might still want to change their minds and keep their babies. The way we do this is with non-judgmental signs and handing out appropriate gifts and infor-mational materials.

On this particular crisp, sunny fall day, I parked down the street from the building as usual and loaded my arms with signs, gifts and materials to hand out. When I looked over at the "sidewalk" where we normally stand by the driveway, I saw that already three women were gathered. I was expecting my sweet

Catholic friend Ingrid to still be there, as her shift as an advocate for the unborn was about to end; she's in her seventies and slightly frail, having recently recovered from cancer. My friend Janet, who goes to my nondenominational Protestant church, would arrive soon to begin our shift as advocates, but I didn't know the other two women standing close to Ingrid. As I approached her, I could see something was not right. What were those loud, shrill noises? Why were the women both yelling at Ingrid, mocking her use of the rosary? Why did that lady in a plaid shirt just throw Ingrid's pro-life sign down on the ground? Why was the other one with short hair videoing us with her phone?

Ingrid looked sad and frazzled, but she continued to replace her signs that were being uprooted and tossed about by the angry protestors. They yelled, "Why do you hate women?" "Why do you come here?" "Why don't you just go home?" I could not comprehend the antagonistic uproar they created, so I proceeded as normal to prepare my spot by the fence, where I would pray and share baby gifts and other items with the women who came to the abortion clinic. I had new baby hats, socks, and blankets for the pregnant mothers, with scriptures, candy, and even pieces of jewelry, all in sealed, see-through plastic bags. The two women rounded on me as I unpacked the gifts and brochures and placed the "Ask to See Your Ultrasound" and "AbortionPillReversal.com" signs on the other side of the driveway. My heart raced as I said to them, "Good morning, would you like a present?" I took out a new  bracelet and offered it to the smaller woman, and she muttered, "Yes," grabbed it from my hand, and threw it down into the dirt. As I picked up the bracelet, I realized: there was no reasoning with them—they were committed to a non-stop verbal assault against us.

The tall woman lit a cigarette, walked much too close to me, and exhaled smoke right into my face.

She ranted fiercely, "These women have free will to do what they want with their bodies. God gave us free will; you should know that. But you think you're better than God, just because you think you can tell women what to do with their bodies. What makes you better than God? What makes you think you can tell women what to do with their bodies, even though God says nothing about it? NOTHING! Maybe it's guilt? You're here to harass them." They both kept yelling these accusations at me, filming me all the while. At least they were finally leaving poor Ingrid alone.

I no longer answered them, but clutched my clipboard closer to my body. My clipboard had ruled notebook paper on the other side for me to write the date and notes of anything significant that I wanted to remember from that day; the other side had a large message reading, "Hi! ☺ Can I help you?" to display to people driving in. There was also a little address label I had pasted on my clipboard when I was in school years before, just in case it got lost. The short one moved in close enough to see and video it. She read out loud my full name and home address while videoing. Then she told me, "I'm going to send you hate mail like you send to the women who come in here." (Now, to be very clear, I've never sent hate mail to anyone, let alone would I want to or even have a way of knowing *how* to send hate mail to women who drive into an abortion clinic! My sole purpose is to love and encourage the women who come hoping to find a solution to their problem.) She continued, "The irony of coming here to harass people and then being scared when you're being harassed." Then she let out a loud "Whoop!"

As I waited anxiously for Janet's arrival, I filmed their antics and texted Janet.

> Do not talk to the two pro-choice women when you get here because they aren't friendly to our cause, and it won't do any good to interact with them.

Unfortunately, Janet did not get my text, and she was caught unaware of the troubling situation she faced. They moved in on Janet and asked, "What's your name?" She answered them, but then they kept hurtling questions that became jumbled words. "How do you call yourself a Christian, coming out and harassing these women? Another Christian who doesn't love people—you're here to spread hate! You're harassing them into changing their minds! You're shaming them and making them feel bad over something they shouldn't feel bad about! They come here for help. You just need to go home!"

The short one asked sarcastically, "How do you sleep at night?" Janet held her ground and in a quiet, strong voice, said, "Look into my eyes—I sleep very well."

They moved away at that point, and soon Ingrid left, but the pro-aborts continued to taunt us for about half an hour before they finally left also. As they hurried away, they slowed down to uproot my signs and threw them as far as they could. We breathed a sigh of relief, at least until the next day....

2

The Conflict of Opposing Perspectives and Beliefs

Cling tightly to your faith in Christ and always keep your conscience clear, doing what you know is right. For some people have disobeyed their consciences and deliberately done what they knew was wrong.

1 Timothy 1:19

The government says abortion is legal, and the church remains silent on the topic, so people think, "Why not do it?"

—Jack Asher

Shiela writing:

Why do some people believe that helping women who are facing one of the toughest choices of their lives is wrong? Who decided as a society that abortion is so often the best choice for a woman facing an unplanned pregnancy? And how did our society become so convoluted that we decided as a nation to legalize abortion? What are Christians to believe about this monumental topic? What are we called to do, if anything?

The evil of abortion (including infanticide) is not a new concept to our day and age. Throughout ancient history, human life was not highly valued by pagans. The Bible has multiple references about sanctity of life—or lack thereof. In battles, invading soldiers would rip open pregnant women's bodies to kill them and their children.[7] In the Bible's Old Testament, Scripture discloses that a person was charged with two counts of manslaughter if someone killed a mother and her baby in the womb.[8] Pagans would sacrifice infants by fire to appease their false gods. This human sacrifice was detestable to God. He commanded His people to destroy those who worshiped in this wicked way.[9] Male infanticide was practiced in Egypt by Pharaoh in the era in which Moses was born,[10] and again it was ordered by King Herod in Judea after Christ was born.[11]

Modern-Day Dilemmas

All humans are made in God's glorious image, and we all are blessed to have some of His wonderful attributes as well. To erase a life He has created is to wipe out a part of His creation. He loves all of His children equally, no matter the age. But our churches are not preaching that abortion is sin, and our United States government has decided it is legal, so people for decades now are thinking, *What could be wrong with it?*

The United States is among just six other countries that allow abortion up to the time of a baby's birth—Canada, China, the Netherlands, North Korea, Singapore, and Vietnam. How sad that our country is lumped in with Communist and Socialist nations which do not value life created in God's image.

Christians believe human life is a miracle from conception. In a discussion with my teenage daughter, she pointed out that if some living, growing cells were found on another planet, it would be considered one of the greatest discoveries of all time. A mother's womb should be the safest place on planet earth. Yet, abortion, which is deliberate destruction of life, far too often is considered a "right" conferred only on the woman. The child she carries in her womb is granted no right to life.

Very simply, science proves that life begins at conception, when the sperm gametes meet the egg, forming a brand-new cell called a zygote. It's a miracle that the two join despite multiple potential barriers, even in ideal circumstances. Upon meeting, they instantly form brand-new DNA in that zygote. At that point, a miraculous zinc spark[12] occurs: the egg is fertilized, and cell division begins, forming a blastocyst that implants in the uterine wall. There a human being is nourished and grows in the mother's womb, its safe place. To extinguish that new cellular bundle on purpose is to kill a life created by God, which is tantamount to declaring that we are superior to our omnipotent Father.

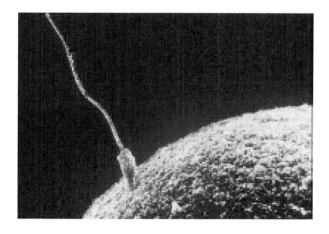

Photo of conception when the sperm penetrates the egg

I am originally from Oregon, one of the first states to pass a very liberal abortion law in 1969, just two years before I was born. (Thank God my pregnant, distressed mother did not abort me, but at that time the husband's consent was required, and she knew my father would never agree.) The law allowed abortion for several reasons, including posing a substantial risk to the physical or mental health of the mother. Please realize, this doesn't mean the pregnant girl or woman had to be severely schizophrenic; it could be something as simple as the mother-to-be thinking she'd be emotionally too upset to continue with the pregnancy. Other approved reasons to abort were rape, incest, physical risk to the mother, or a potentially handicapped baby.

Soon after, in 1973, Roe v. Wade[13] and Doe v. Bolton[14] had the combined effect that federal law allowed abortion to be available on demand from conception to birth. It was nearly 20 years before federal judges allowed states to pass their own pro-life restrictions, but Oregon was the only state that never did. In fact, taxpayers in Oregon now fund free abortions on demand.[15]

Even more disturbing, in January 2019, Governor Cuomo of New York pushed through the Reproductive Health Act so that if Roe v. Wade was repealed federally, his state could still have legal abortions. With the Act passed, abortions would be easily available on demand up to 24 weeks, even by non-doctors, and up to birth for certain reasons. And a baby-killing in a woman's womb would no longer be considered a homicide. When the law was passed, the New York state legislature applauded and cheered for joy, and their liberal governor (who was sporting a pink tie) was so proud that he had the spire on the One World Trade Center building, along with certain other landmarks, lit up in pink lights to celebrate their "victory."

When I heard about this New York celebration, I was appalled. I've been in pro-life circles for years and have conservative social media friends; however, I've been shocked to find that New York's new law is not common knowledge and has not been on the evening news. I spoke with a recent graduate from a Christian university who described herself as pro-choice (she personally would feel uncomfortable with it but didn't want to impose her own views onto other women). I asked, "What do you think of New York's laws passed earlier this year [2019]?"

She answered, "I don't know what laws for abortion they have there—what are they?"

I took the opportunity to educate her. "It's legal there to abort all the way up to birth."

"Oh, wow," she answered. "I didn't know that happened anywhere in the U.S."

I had almost the identical conversation with an older mother of two adults who also was completely shocked and appalled when I mentioned the law to her, even though she's a conservative Catholic. The news media knows that the majority of Americans don't approve of full-term abortions, so they don't publicize these "progressive" laws. It is not okay that Christians don't know what's happening right here in the United States!

We might expect that Oregon and New York have pro-choice legislation, but they aren't the only ones. There are actually a handful of states that also allow abortion up until birth for certain reasons, Massachusetts being among the newest in December 2020; their bill also includes lowering the legal age for teenagers to have an abortion without parental consent to 16. Full-term abortion is also legal in Alaska, Colorado, New Hampshire, New Jersey, New Mexico, Vermont, and Washington, D.C. Are *you* aware of the pro-choice and pro-life laws in your own state? Inform yourself—the information is very easy to find.[16]

> *My people are destroyed from lack of knowledge.*
> *Hosea 4:6 (NIV)*

3

The Pro-Life Movement in Greenville, South Carolina

Remember, it is sin to know what you ought to do and then not do it.

James 4:17 (NLT)

The only thing necessary for the triumph of evil is for good men to do nothing.

—Attributed to Edmund Burke

Shiela writing:

I have been privileged to follow in the steps of thousands of pro-lifers who have gone before me here in upstate South Carolina. The concept of an abortion bothered them; they knew Roe v. Wade was contrary to God's law, and instead of just thinking and worrying about it, they advocated for a child's right to life and decided to take action. One of my mentors on the sidewalk has been pro-life advocate Anne Huff, who wrote *The Awakening, The Pro-Life Movement in South Carolina, Learning from the Past to Shape the Future.* She did a fabulous job of encapsulating much of the pro-lifers' activities, the legislative efforts, and related news stories from this area over the past 30-plus years. I have gleaned some points to highlight from her book (quoted and/or paraphrased) in the remainder of this chapter, with her permission.

The Awakening

The year was 1988 and George H.W. Bush was president. God began to speak to the hearts of men and women all over the U.S.A...[about] a plan to awaken our nation to the reality of the evil intention to destroy the Biblical foundation of our country. These people eagerly received what the Holy Spirit was speaking to their hearts and determined to run to the battle.

In July, a movement began to engage in peaceful protest at abortion clinics around Atlanta, Georgia. Located just a few hours away, some South Carolinians felt drawn to participate. The pro-testors were instructed to maintain a high standard code of conduct: "passive resistance on their hands and knees, in silence."[17] They did not leave the clinic when ordered to do so by the police. Some instead went limp as they were carried away, arrested, and sometimes beaten, as they were hauled off to jail. The South Carolinians left Atlanta resolute to start a similar movement in the Upstate.

There had been peaceful protests by pro-life advocates in years past, but without recognizable results, so advocates, including those in Upstate South Carolina, planned to begin "rescue style" protests, following the Atlanta model of a sit-in. A rescue is "when a person places his own body between an unborn child and the people who want to take the life of that child."[18]

The protest would involve trespassing: sitting down in front of the abortion clinic doors or on the driveway to block people's access. They purposefully planned to be passive and not resist the police. Participants like Betty Walsh felt it was wrong "as a Christian to sit back and do nothing.... Our God was calling us to battle, and we looked forward to getting on with the mission. This is our way of telling God we are sorry for what is going on at these clinics. But what we are saying in the marches and protests is that God's law is above man's law, and we must obey God's law.... All the letter writing to congressmen, governors and everybody else has not changed their minds, so we feel the civil protests are the way to stop abortions; so-called civil unrest is a very Biblical stand...."[19]

Pro-life groups communicated with the media before their protests "to reassure people that the demonstrations would be conducted in a Christian manner with the goal of preventing the murder of innocent preborn babies." This new style sparked debates amongst many local Christian leaders, but what advocates had been trying so far hadn't worked, so this "Operation Rescue" was seen as a new strategy.[20]

Beginning February 1989, there were multiple sit-ins at the three Greenville abortion clinics, resulting in hundreds of pro-lifers being arrested and/or fined. By all accounts, pro-lifers remained peaceful while trespassing. There is a law in South Carolina that if you trespass to save a life, then you didn't do anything wrong. That is the argument they used in court—trespassing to save lives.[21]

Pro-life attorney, Doug Churdar, argued that "just because something is legal doesn't mean it is right." Laws change. Slavery, for instance, was once legal. "One day, history will vindicate those who had the guts and backbone to risk arrest and humiliation to stop abortion." He also argued that this movement is similar to those of people who had stood against the atrocities of slavery, the Holocaust and women's suffrage. He stated that none of those wrongs would have been corrected without people taking a stand for their beliefs.[22]

Some trespassers were jailed multiple times, as was Anne Schell, who said the following:

As long as babies are being killed, we will stand up for them. Somebody has to speak for them, and that's what we are doing. If the children were heard crying as they were being torn apart, it would really make a difference. We are telling God that we don't agree with what is going on at abortion clinics. One day, everybody is going to have to answer when God asks, "What did you do to stop abortion?" I want to be able to answer I did everything I could…. Our children and grandchildren need to see us crying out on behalf of their generation, a generation that is being slaughtered en masse. There is so much at stake—their very future is in our hands.

What does it say to our young people if we adults do not think it is important enough to at least come out for one or two hours a month to pray outside [an abortion clinic]? Someday we may wish our children would stand up for us. But they will never see it as a priority if they have not seen us making it a priority in our lives. Indeed, why should they, if they don't see us setting the example before them? No one can take your place…we must keep pressing toward the prize and be a witness for Christ.

Our message is that we are there for women in need — whether a woman needs advice, money to have her baby, a reference for an adoption agency, or even if she makes what we consider to be the wrong choice by going through with the abortion. [23]

Richard Cash, who went on to become District 3 S.C. State Senator, was arrested multiple times over the years in Boston and Greenville during peaceful protests outside of abortion clinics. He said, "I have the courage to stand up for what I believe at personal cost to myself and I will fight for what I believe in even if it seems unpopular."[24]

As the sit-in protests continued in the Upstate, hundreds of protestors were arrested, fined, and/or jailed as a result of the "rescue" movement. Whether you agree or not with the tactics, the result of the rescues was to bring the pro-life issue to the forefront of legal and legislative activity. Illegal picketing ordinances were abolished and protestors' rights were established and recognized. Droves of pastors, churches and congregants became involved over the next few years, and the pro-life movement was revitalized. And meanwhile, through it all, sidewalk counseling never stopped taking place.

Dr. Robert Jackson, a Spartanburg physician, said he frequently saw pregnant women trying to decide what outcome to choose. He stated, "I don't minimize their situations, but there are no circumstances desperate enough to require abortion; I don't believe in situational ethics."[25]

Around the early 90s there seemed to be an overall shift in the movement. In 1993, at the site of my (Shiela's) current church in Greenville, there was a large rally attended by about 1,500 pro-lifers. The rally's theme encouraged everyone to continue protesting, but emphasized they do it peacefully and prayerfully without yelling or any violence.

By that time, three abortion clinics had been opened in Greenville. After one abortionist died in an auto accident in 1995, his clinic closed; the second clinic shut down due to financial reasons when S.C. state legislators enacted new procedures. That left one abortion clinic in business, but the facility was located in a secluded, fenced area near the Greenville hospital.

It was a challenging location to offer information to women going in. There was no place where a driver could pull over to talk. Conversations were often cut short because of someone pulling up behind the stopped car wanting to get into the clinic. Through prayer and fasting, pro-lifers were eventually able to open a pregnancy resource center right next door to this clinic.

The two abortion doctors at this clinic no doubt were frustrated with the amount of activity by pro-lifers over the years. At one point, they had their landscapers cover the ground with horse manure so that the pro-lifers had nowhere to stand. That fragrant plan was foiled brilliantly by a pro-lifer who hurried to a nearby hardware store and bought some drop cloths. She carefully laid the drop cloths over the manure and they continued to minister as usual.

Multiple pro-life groups started up in Greenville over the years; some were organic to the area, and some were connected on a national level. Greenville for Life,[26] a local umbrella organization for the various pro-life groups in the area, began meeting officially in 2014.

Part Two

Settling on Opposite Sides of the Fence

4

Dionne's Background

Children's children are a crown to the aged, and parents are the pride of their children.

Proverbs 17:6 (NIV)

Dionne writing:

My daddy was a mechanic and my momma was a stay-at-home mom. She took care of me and my brother and she cooked and cleaned. Every Friday when my daddy got off work, we would load up the family into the car and travel nearly an hour south to Greenwood; he felt like since we spent the week here in Greenville, we should visit with relatives for the weekend. After attending Baptist church with my grandmomma, we'd come back home on Sunday afternoon.

One clear winter evening, when I was just shy of my second birthday, we once again loaded up the car and took off towards Greenwood. It was my daddy, my momma, my brother Rob, who was four, and myself in the car. It was winter and dark already, but it was clear and not too cold. My brother and I had no idea what was happening when suddenly, there was a loud noise and jolt as another car hit us, running us off the road. Our car quickly became airborne, flipped, and landed upside-down with a crash. The front windshield shattered from the impact, and there was glass every-where.

"Jean," my father yelled, "Are you all right?" There was no answer from my mother, because she was unconscious. My father rushed to open his door; I was behind him, so he pulled me out first, then raced around the car to the other side to get my brother Rob, then pulled Momma out. He was working fast and hard, so that's probably why he bled out so fast. Nobody had even known my father was hurt, because he was just focused on getting us out of the car, which he did. In this one last selfless act, he got us all out to safety on the nearby embankment. As we waited for the ambulance to arrive, my father bled to death. A piece of glass hit an artery in his neck, and he bled out. Nobody saw it in the dark, and he died before the ambulance came. I was fine, but they had to remove glass out of my brother's forehead; mom had a concussion. We all stayed overnight in the hospital.

Dionne's Father

It took us a while to bounce back from losing my father. After the car accident, eventually my momma decided it was time to go to work. For years she worked at a nursing home, and I guess I was six years old when she started working for Dr. Two a couple days a week, helping his wife take care of the baby she'd just had.

That's how my mom got in touch with the abortion doctor and got to know him and his family. We started spending time up there—his kids, my momma's kids. We would go on vacations together, and then, eventually, she started working at the clinic on the weekend. Because—I don't think a lot of people know—in the beginning they were only doing procedures on Fridays and Saturdays. So that cut out some of the times worked at the nursing home, and that was great for us; it meant she would be home in the evenings Fridays and Saturdays. We had our uncle and other family members, but it's nothing like our mom. She's special. So eventually, they added another day, so those three days she was at the clinic for a few years. Probably the late 90s is when they started [abortions] every day, Monday through Saturday.

Becoming an Abortion Worker

As we got older, my mom started doing more traveling, since she didn't have small children to take care of. She and her friends were going on cruises and other trips, so that's when she asked me if I wanted to cover weekends for her. And at that time, I wasn't working on the weekend. I was basically working Monday through Thursday, so I said, "Sure, why not?" I started working every blue moon, probably once every three months or so. I didn't start at the clinic until 2003. And then I became full-time there in 2005 after my mom had to have open heart surgery. My brother and I forced her to go into retirement. I think that was probably the best thing for my mom, and the worst thing for her. I'm the only girl. I have three brothers, and they're a pain in the butt!

Sometimes I think if I had to do it over again, I probably would have gone the same route: I would have taken this job. But sometimes I get an uneasy feeling working at the clinic when I listen to some of the ladies talk about what they've been through. I'm not used to that. I mean, I've always had the support of my family, and I just don't understand how some families are not as tight-knit as mine. I never understood it. I know, now, that everybody's family is not the same. Some people can't talk to their family members. They have no one to talk to, so they feel like this is the only option they have, when in reality it's not—there are always other options out there. You've just got to know where to look and who to talk to.

You get these people that tell you, "Well, if you have that baby, that's going to mess up your life. You're not going to be able to do what you want." Man, I was able to have both of my pregnancies; I could go to school, go to work, and still take care of my children. It's all about what you know you're capable of doing, and just because it was easy for me doesn't mean it's going to be easy for you. But anything that's worth having doesn't come easy. And the child is meant to be here; you got pregnant for a reason, because it was meant to be.

Raising My Own Children

I've always felt like I wasn't the marrying kind, because I felt nobody would be as faithful as I am in a relationship. However, I did have a desire to have children. Even when I was a teenager, I had a plan to have a girl first and then a boy, and I always wanted them to be three years apart. And that's exactly what ended up happening, even though neither pregnancy was intentionally planned at the time. Abortion never even crossed my mind when I became pregnant with either of my children.

My daughter's father was lucky to even know about my child, because I had no intentions of telling him that I was pregnant. I had made up my mind I was going to have my child, and I didn't need him. But my momma sat me down and told me, "He needs to know. You need to give him the opportunity to step up and be a father for your daughter." And I said, "Why? I don't need him." She told me, "It doesn't have anything to do with what you need. He has the right to know, and that child has a right to know her father." So, I figured, okay, whatever. I called him up and told him that I needed to talk to him. Right off the bat I said, "I'm not telling you this because I want anything from you, or need anything from you; I'm telling you because I figured you had the right to know. I'm pregnant, and I'm having it, regardless of what you think or don't think. I don't really care." And he told me that he would support me with whatever I decided. I told him, "I already told you I'm going to have my baby regardless of the situation." And I have to admit, he was a stand-up dude; he was supportive, and he even proposed. I told him, "Man, don't even think about it. I'm not telling you this because I want anything from you. I'm telling you because you have a right to know. What you do with that information is totally up to you. You can either step up and be a father or you can be a dead-beat. Regardless of what you do, my baby will not want for anything." And she never did want for anything. In a way I'm glad I did tell him, because it was beneficial for my daughter, Demetria, to know him and his family before he passed away a few years ago, God rest his soul.

Although neither baby was planned, my son was most *definitely* not planned. His father and I have always been best friends. I told him right off the bat that I was pregnant, not caring if he was happy or not. He already had other children, but Desmond was his first son. And I don't know why he also felt like, since I was having his child, he wanted to propose. I told him, "No, I don't want to marry you; that's not why I'm keeping this child. I'm not trying to hold on to you. I got pregnant, and I'm going to deal with this situation. I'm going to keep my child. I'm going to raise it—that doesn't mean I want to marry you. I really would like you to be a part of your child's life. That doesn't mean I want you." We stayed good friends, and he has been a part of my son's life.

I knew I didn't need to marry either one of them to raise a child, because I have an aunt that works at the OB clinic; I knew that there are options available out there because we were raised and taught about them. My daddy died at a young age, and my momma raised us by herself. She had help from my aunts and my grandparents, but at the end of the day, it was her raising us. And if I do say so myself, she did a doggone good job. I had told myself that if I had any kids, that would be me. I thought, "I can do this myself, if my momma can do it," and it was ten times harder then than it is now, so there's no excuse.

Continuing as an Abortion Worker

I started at the clinic in 2003 to be a fill-in for my mom when she needed some extra help. Here it is 18 years later, and I'm still there. I can't really say why I'm still there; I guess it's almost like when you're in a relationship and you feel comfortable and you're scared to venture out. That's where I'm at now. It's not like I don't have the degrees to have something else. I do, but I'm comfortable with the people that I work with. Somewhat like a relationship, when you get comfortable, leaving scares you, and it scares me to undertake a new endeavor. But I do sometimes think that there's something else I'm meant to do besides working there.

Some people think that since I, my mom, and my aunt worked there, and now my daughter works there, that we all must really believe in abortion and that our family must have had a lot of them. Believe it or not, none of us believe in abortion, but we believe in a woman's right to choose what she wants to do. I can honestly say that in my entire family, we've only had two people that have come in there to have an abortion. I told both relatives that I would adopt their babies if they would just keep them. Each time, I was willing to have an open adoption; they could come whenever they wanted so the child would know who their parent was—I wouldn't keep that from them. They went through with it anyway, and I was livid, but it wasn't my decision. I can't tell them what to do or not do; all I can do is to give them my opinion. Since they were family, I was really able to voice my opinion about the decision; but at the end of the day, they still did what they wanted to do. Some folks already have their mind made up regardless of what anybody says or does.

I get asked a lot how I can work here. I don't know—sometimes I ask myself that and I still haven't come up with an answer. It's a job. And it pays my bills. And I like the people that I work with, and the people that I work for. The ones that actually know what I do ask me, "How can you do what you do?" It's hard. That I will not lie about. It's hard, because I am the one that weighs the fetus once it is suctioned out. I weigh it, and sometimes it's hard. Some are harder to do than others. I say that because the ones that are early in the pregnancy, are more like a blood clot, so it's nothing really discernible. But the ones that are farther along, and there are pieces—that's a baby. Now those…those are a little harder to do. But I suck it up and I think about my kids. They're here, they're healthy, and I know that's something I would never do to mine. Even if I got pregnant today, which is impossible, but let's just say it happened, I would have my child. When two of my co-workers were pregnant, they would be asked, "How can you be pregnant and working in an abortion clinic?" And they told them, "Well, this is my job, but to have my baby is my choice, and I'm going to have my baby, regardless of where I work."

When my daughter was in high school, I had her come to the clinic on one of their off days, because I wanted her to see what some of these girls go through and the emotion that it can have on them. I wasn't trying to be cruel; I wanted her to be educated about her options and let her know that this is something I would never ask of her. I told her, "I wouldn't make you do something you wouldn't want to do, and I wouldn't talk you out of doing some-thing you wanted to do. But I would be ticked if you had an abortion. At the end of the day, it's not my choice, it's yours."

So I had her come visit, and she got a lot out of it. After that day, she said, "Mama, I would never, ever have an abortion, because I wouldn't want to put myself through anything like that." And I said, "Well, I'm glad to hear that." And then a few months later, her friends came to me and asked me about the abortion clinic and the effects that it has on some girls. I said, "Well, a lot of young girls like you are forced because their parents don't want them to have any kids, and if they did, then they would be put out and everything. There are other options out there if you get pregnant. There's too much help out there to actually abort a child, but at the end of the day, it's y'all's choice." And I can say that none of my daughter's friends had any kids while they were in high school. When they got older, they didn't have any abortions, and the ones that did get pregnant had their children. I like to say that I had a little bit to do with that.

Back in 2005, after two years, I came close to leaving the clinic. I was going through a lot of things, and in that state of mind, it was difficult to work with the public. My grandma had passed away on Christmas Eve of that year, and I had told myself that I wasn't going to do it anymore, that I was going to walk away in 2006. I was going to do something else with my education. I even thought about going back to the restaurants, being a manager again.

I don't know; I was in a totally different place when my grandma passed; it hit me so hard that I didn't even want to deal with anybody. I even pulled away from my own children for a while. It took Dr. Two to sit down and talk to me, and he realized what I was going through. He told me that if I never stepped foot back into the clinic that he would understand, and that no matter what, he would have my back on whatever I decided I was going to do. I appreciated that, because it was a very hard time in my life. Believe it or not, her death still affects me and a lot of my family to this day at Christmastime. I had small kids then, so we still celebrated it, but our hearts weren't in it. After that, things just happened, and I did go back to the clinic. Then it was like the years started flying by, and in March 2021 it was 18 years. My kids are grown, and I have a grandchild now.

When my son told me that he got his girlfriend pregnant, I said, "For real?" That's the first thing that came out of my mouth. I figured, *Okay, so I'm going to be a grandmother*. I said, "Well, at least you all waited until I was in my late forties and not a young grandmother." I wasn't a young mother, so I'm not like some of these other folks that want to start at 16, 17 to have kids. I waited until I was 25. But that's a whole different category because I didn't want kids, but then I did. I can truthfully say, I love that little grandbaby like she was my own. I'm still not understanding where she gets "Gra" from, but it's kind of grown on me. I don't think I would want to be called Grandma now. I like Gra. It's wild. It's crazy, but it's cool. I enjoy being a grandmother just as much as I enjoy being a mother. I'm glad I had that experience.

Children are a gift from the LORD; they are a reward from him.

Psalm 127:3 (NLT)

5

Shiela's Background

I advise you to obey only the Holy Spirit's instructions. He will tell you where to go and what to do.

Galatians 5:16

Shiela writing:

The miraculous account of my birth—and my mother's change of heart—is recounted in full in my book *Memoirs of a Miracle Baby, A Testimony of God's Love,*[27] a story of how I, as a breech baby, was born clinically dead in a chiropractor's office. The chiropractor and his nurse tried everything they could to revive me, but they weren't able to wake me up. Despairing of my life, the doctor handed me to my mother, urging, "Evelyn, we've tried everything—you'll have to see if you can revive her by getting her to nurse." When my mother first laid eyes on my lifeless, blue body, she fell in love. She said, "You had the most beautiful little face I'd ever seen," and she could not bear the thought of burying me. Months of frustration, despair, devastation, and anger at being pregnant evaporated in that moment; she wanted only that I should live, and she pleaded to God in a way that she never had before. Then, she

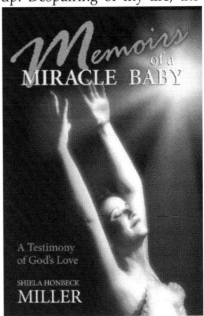

31

told me, "You began to nurse like your little life depended on it," and the color returned to my body.

The relief extended beyond my mother and those attending the birth to my family members and church family, who had all been enlisted to pray on our behalf that night. Though the chiropractor was sure that I would have severe intellectual disabilities resulting from the lack of oxygen at my birth, I grew and developed without any congenital problems or disabilities of any kind. I truly was a miracle baby.

The experience completely transformed my mother. She felt a surge of life and energy, not to mention a new perspective: she had purpose now, and both her body and spirit felt rejuvenated. Fears dissipated and confidence emerged. My sister, who was fourteen when I was born, told me that everything seemed to change for Mom at that time. Mom told her family that it was the best thing she ever did, the best choice she ever made. She felt that I gave her more energy and desire to live than anything else in her life. I—the baby she had not wanted, the baby she could have aborted—became her greatest joy.

In retrospect, it seems obvious that I should have become a pro-life advocate. God not only saved my life but my mother's as well. Ours is a powerful testimony of His grace and power to rescue both child and mother, even through awful circumstances. But standing outside an abortion clinic, waving down cars and trying to convince scared pregnant women in ten seconds why they should take some time to listen to me urge them not to abort their babies is not anything I ever imagined I would do with the miraculous life God gave me. In fact, he had a few more life events for me to experience to help me prepare for that particular ministry.

Becoming Foster Parents

Pure and genuine religion in the sight of God the Father means caring for orphans and widows in their distress and refusing to let the world corrupt you.

James 1:27 (NLT)

One pleasant fall day in 2013, I was helping my daughter go door to door with her yearly American Heritage Girls scouting fundraiser in our neighborhood.

"How many more houses do you want to go to today?" I asked Sydney.

"Let's try to finish all the houses on this street, because I want to win Top Seller badge this year," she decided.

We were just about to knock on a neighbor's door when we heard a loud commotion across the street. We both immediately looked over to see an angry man shaking his fists and yelling in his driveway at a weeping teenage girl, probably his daughter, who was cowering away from him. We were horrified to see him start whipping her violently with his belt as she tried futilely to dodge his blows raining down on her body. The young girl fell to her knees. She begged him to stop hitting her, but he just yelled, "If you think this is bad, you haven't seen anything!" She scrambled into their car; he climbed into the driver's seat and quickly drove away.

Our neighbors told us they had previously witnessed a similarly disturbing incident and had called the authorities on that father. That family soon ended up moving away from our neighborhood, but the violent episode continued to haunt me and Sydney.

It so bothered me that the next morning in worship at church I was crying. I asked God, "How will a child come to know Your Fatherly love if that child has endured horrendous abuse from an earthly father?" God's answer was revealed to me through His words that came into my head: *You foster.*

He wanted my husband and me to become foster parents. We already had two young and active children to rear. But I knew it was something our family was meant to do. And as usually happens when God is behind changing our lives, everything eventually fell into place with His timing. Sydney, who had been deeply affected at the sight of the angry father abusing the daughter, kept pestering me as the months passed, asking repeatedly, "When are we going to foster?" She was excited about the prospect of welcoming a sister. My husband had already warmed to the idea; he had suggested foster parenting a couple of years earlier, but I had been reluctant because I thought it would be too painful when the foster children left. I finally understood that it would be worth the radical temporary change in our family life to be able to show children God's love and kindness.

I had a lot going on during that period, and it took some time to become licensed foster parents. My book was finished that same fall, but I still needed to finish school to become a physical therapist assistant. I graduated that next year, in October 2014. Sadly, my father passed away in Oregon in January 2015; thankfully, I was able to visit with him the Thanksgiving beforehand. My husband and I traveled to his memorial service that February, at which I read the chapter in my book dedicated to him and performed a worship dance.[28] His death hit me hard, and it took some time to recover. I don't know that one ever fully recovers when a loved one dies, but Christians are blessed by their faith in the Lord.

That very next weekend was my church women's retreat, and I journaled what I heard the Holy Spirit telling me. Here are just a few excerpts from that personal encounter:

I was with your Daddy, and he felt My presence and knew he was coming to join Me. He loved you so much, his baby—his special miracle baby. He was so proud of you, Shiela. He was My precious son, and I granted him much peace. His prayers for you and yours for him were sweet to Me as sweet incense. He was faithful and true to Me and spent time with Me daily. You are following in his example. I saved you when you were born. Your father didn't even know you yet and he loved you. I heeded his cries on your behalf. He was a righteous man, and I honored his fervent requests and prayers to Me. I formed you in the womb, specially, custom made. I know all your flaws and imperfections, and I love you just the same. I'm your Daddy. It's been a blessing bestowed upon you to have had your earthly daddy because I have a special bond with you. You are not an orphan now. You are not fatherless. I am your Comforter. I care so much for you that I orchestrated timing of these events for you. My timing is perfect. My love covers all.

No, my earthly dad wasn't perfect, but God foreordained that he was the perfect dad for me and my siblings. He knew what we would need to become mature, loving adults.

Meanwhile, I started working as a physical therapist assistant, and we finally started the foster licensing process in 2015, finishing in early 2016. We welcomed two elementary-age siblings into our home that spring. We had to be careful to safeguard their identities, but I did a television interview with Sydney and discussed as much as possible to share our story and encourage others to foster. It's also the one time that Sydney danced with me on television, and it was a memory that I'll always treasure.[29]

That was a challenging but very rewarding season for our family, jumping from two children to four. We kept busy with a lot of activities, taking them to new places so they could have fun experiences, like their first pony rides and a giant birthday party. Our family offered them a safe, stable, loving environment; they each accepted Jesus as their Savior and were baptized during their last summer with us. Saying good-bye to our foster children was one of the hardest things we've ever done, because we were so sad when they left for their next home, but we had 16 months' worth of happy memories that we will always cherish.

After our season of fostering had ended, I kept wondering what God wanted me to do next. Could it really be sidewalk counseling? It was a season to meditate on Him and His words to me.

> Don't act thoughtlessly, but try to find out and do whatever the Lord wants you to.
>
> Ephesians 5:17

> He is my father's God and mine, and my only purpose in life is to please him.
>
> 2 Timothy 1:3

Becoming a Pro-Life Activist

So let's not get tired of doing what is good. At just the right time we will reap a harvest of blessing if we don't give up.

Galatians 6:9 (NLT)

Be sure to carry out the ministry the Lord gave you.

Colossians 4:17 (NLT)

I'm definitely not the type of person that runs towards confrontation, and I did not suddenly wake up one day and decide to become a pro-life activist. I am actually an introvert. I had never protested anything in my life, and, frankly, wasn't interested in what I thought was a scary movement. Holding signs and protesting a law? I did have friends who were so pro-life that as a regular part of their lifestyle, they would boycott certain brands and stores that "charitably" funded abortion. They knew scads of related statistics and also what was happening on national and global levels with horror stories of fetuses being used in immoral ways. I felt I was just a "regular" Christian who didn't feel abortion was right except in the case of rape and/or incest; it *was* legal, so who was I to try to stop women from making that choice? And I assumed hormonal birth control was all right as well; I mean, isn't that what everyone respectable and educated did if they really didn't want to get pregnant? That's what I was taught back in the early 90s in my Christian university's early parenting class.

If anyone had lost a child to abortion in my large extended family, it was a well-kept secret, even to this day; regardless, we definitely didn't discuss the topic in our Christian home. For a while, it seemed that Christians ignored the issue. I certainly did not hear about it in church growing up. I was around two when Roe v. Wade occurred, and abortion was already legal in Oregon if it was considered physically or emotionally traumatic for the mother to continue the pregnancy. I barely ever had abortion cross my radar, except as a teenager and once again as an adult. When I turned 14, a dance classmate of mine had a baby on her 16th birthday. Her parents were staunch Catholics, and although they didn't approve of her actions causing her to become pregnant, they lovingly supported her in keeping the baby. However, another classmate, who was 21, told us about her experience having two dilation and curettage procedures, also called D&C abortions.[30] She openly explained the procedure while expressing no obvious feeling or emotion: "The doctor used suction and then scraped out the inside of my uterus. It was uncomfortable, but I'll probably end up doing it again the next time I get pregnant." She wasn't a very friendly person, and she seemed rather cold-hearted about the whole ordeal, but she just didn't want children at that time and considered it a reasonable method of birth control. As a young teen, I remember thinking that sounded like a horrible thing to do to your body, not to mention what it did to the baby.

When I was around age 30 and living in Reno, Nevada, my medical terminology teacher took it upon himself to explain to us what a partial-birth abortion consisted of. With graphic details, he showed us how a developed baby in the womb could be stabbed in the neck, then ripped apart, being pulled out piece by piece. Our class was horrified, and at least one classmate was verbally upset with him for sharing the details. How evil and sad a procedure it was to terminate a child's life so violently. None of us had any idea that such an atrocity existed.[31]

Living in Greenville, I was now in my mid-forties, and I was so clueless that I didn't even know we had an abortion clinic in our city! So I was completely caught off guard one day at a church event in the fall of 2017, when an acquaintance named Judy had a request to make of me from her friend, Carrie. Judy said, "My friend, Carrie, read your memoir and wants you to create a tri-fold brochure to summarize it so she can hand them out to women outside the abortion clinic." I was astonished, and I asked her why. Judy explained, "Carrie feels that your story is so powerful that it might change some women's minds to keep their babies." With her explanation, I was overcome momentarily with strong emotions, and I had to wipe a tear away. It touched me very deeply, thinking how my story might make a difference and save a life.

I decided to get to know Carrie and find out more details of the ministry she was involved with before I would entrust her with my story. I was amazed with what she told me: she faithfully went every Wednesday morning to pray and to try to talk with women outside the abortion clinic. It sounded very scary, to approach complete strangers about abortion, and I couldn't imagine doing that myself; it was also a major time commitment on her part. My mind was blown that this quiet, soft-spoken woman would stand outside an abortion clinic and talk to complete strangers about their intimate personal decisions, trying to change their minds in life-altering ways. I appreciated her heart for the ministry and created the brochure for her, wishing her well in the endeavor.

The brochure, while based on my book, focused on how joyous my mother had been after I survived a tumultuous birth, even though I had been an unwanted pregnancy. It's an encourage-ment to mothers that they can't yet fathom the full love they'll feel for their unborn child until they get to meet him or her in person.[32]

When we still had our foster children, Carrie kept asking me to come speak and dance at pro-life events, which occurred in the spring and fall. My husband and I knew we were called to be foster parents, and I just didn't see myself getting into the sidewalk counseling as well. I figured the pro-life stuff was for Carrie to do—I honestly was too busy with fostering and working, including on weekends. And if that wasn't enough, my daughter had also become an all-star cheerleader, which required multiple trips to the gym per week and full weekends away at competitions. My time was a precious commodity, so I kept putting off Carrie's invitations. Still, we became friends in the meantime, especially since we were both massage therapists.

Our family schedule calmed down after the foster kids left in 2017. I was at a church conference one weekend that fall, and one of the prophetic speakers told me that he saw me getting involved in a ministry for mothers. I said, "Well, I was a foster mother, so I wonder if it's to those moms?"

But he replied, "No, I really don't think that's it."

"Well, perhaps it has something to do with pro-life ministry?" I inquired.

"Yes, that sounds more along the lines of what I was thinking you were called to do," he answered.

Finally, in spring of 2018, Robert and I had the opportunity to come to our first pro-life event. The timing worked out great, because we had just returned from a fabulous trip to Israel and we had no cheerleading competitions scheduled for that weekend. Now, this event was in a parking lot right next to the abortion clinic, and we hadn't been there before. We accidentally drove up into the driveway of that clinic, and instantly a large man loomed over our low Mustang, loudly proclaiming we shouldn't enter that facility. His exact words escape me, but it was something like, "You don't want to go in there and kill your baby!" The experience was daunting, and I remember thinking, "Dude, we're on your side; give us a break!" We told him we were there to join their group, and we turned around and found another, more suitable place to park.

The rest of our experience that day was great. I told my mother's story based on my book and danced to "How Great the Father's Love." The people were very receptive, and they seemed to enjoy my speech and worship dance, but I still didn't feel convicted to join Carrie outside the abortion clinic. I was in a lull, wondering and waiting for what God had in mind for me to do, but all the while keeping the prophetic man's words in the back of my mind.

Six months later, in mid-August, a local pro-life ministry hosted a training session on how to counsel pregnant women in crisis, and by then I did feel led to go through it. I thought, *This seems like where God is leading me, so I'll give it a shot.* That next week, I went out to the sidewalk with Carrie for the first time. As I now tell all newbies to the sidewalk, "Don't worry about being nervous, because I was scared out of my wits that first day and wouldn't even approach a single car." Thankfully, God knows me well and realized I needed some encouragement to see I was hearing and following Him correctly. That day was amazing, as I will chronicle in the next section, but something else occurred to solidify my calling.

I went to a women's Saturday church event in September 2018. When we returned to our round tables after a break, there was a small blackboard at each place setting. On it, written in chalk, was a unique word. You see, the women who organized the event had prayed over these in our absence and then written the word they felt the Holy Spirit meant for each of us to have. (Please note that it was anonymous; they did not know who was sitting in which seat.) My word was *anointed*. As we took turns explaining our personal word, I shared with my table that I believed it meant I was anointed to do sidewalk ministry. This was confirmed when one of the ladies shared her own abortion experience. "I didn't tell my parents, and all of my friends just said they'd support whatever decision I made, but no one told me that I shouldn't do it, or that it was the wrong decision. There was no one standing outside that day at the abortion clinic for me to stop and talk to, no one to tell me not to do it." She then told me, "Shiela, if you had been there, I wouldn't have gone through with it." This really cemented to me that I need to stand up for these women, to let them know there is someone who believes abortion is the wrong choice, and to give them better alternatives. Hundreds of women pass me without stopping, but at least I can say I was there for them if they had wanted to stop.

The next Saturday was a pro-life event, and I briefly spoke about some wonderful encounters I'd recently had on the sidewalk. Afterwards, Dr. Jackson, who was the keynote speaker, commented, "You had such an enthusiasm when you were talking to us about your interactions with those women—you really have an anointing for this ministry."

Wow, I thought, *God wanted to emphasize the subject of anointing to me. Okay, Lord, I received the message loud and clear.*

The following Saturday, I attended a Christian event and took the opportunity to briefly speak with a local pastor about sidewalk ministry. As we were walking away from each other, he commented, "Great smile."

I murmured, "Maybe that's why they stop for me."

He spun around and asked, "Can I pray for you and your ministry?" I'll give you one guess as to the topic of his prayer, which was yes, to bless the "anointing" on my pro-life ministry work.

Then I thought, *Thank you, God for this triple anointing, I definitely get the message.* He knows me so well—starting out I would question if I were really meant to be in this ministry. I appreciated hearing it the first time. Twice receiving the word could be a coincidence, but I realized that God cared enough to emphasize it to me. But there was no way it was a coincidence after I received it three Saturdays in a row from completely different sources! I knew that I had a special calling and that I had definitely better stay faithful to it! It also spurred me to go to the sidewalk not one but two mornings a week. My work schedule had become more flexible, so going to the sidewalk twice became regularly scheduled events for me every week thereafter.

Months later, in hindsight, a thought finally occurred to me, and I got out my old planner from the previous year. I counted the weeks between when I was given that prophetic word about ministering to mothers and when I took the training to start on the sidewalk. The simple math showed that exactly 40 full weeks were completed, which is the same gestational time period as a full-term baby! And that had been the first local training in quite a while. This demonstrated to me once again that God is good, and we need to trust that His timing is perfect.

Before I formed you in the womb I knew you, before you were born I set you apart.

Jeremiah 1:5 (NIV)

Part Three

Working on Opposite
Sides of the Fence

6

Working Inside the Abortion Clinic

A busy morning inside the secluded abortion facility

Dionne writing:

I'm a night owl, not a morning person, so I usually am the last employee to enter the building. Sometimes I'm the first one in, but typically I get there a few minutes before the doctor does. In the car I listen to my favorite gospel music to get me in the frame of mind I need to be in before I'm around others. Driving in, I see the pro-life protestors lining the driveway, waving and wanting to talk to me. I sometimes wave at them, and if Shiela's there, I stop to chat for a few minutes or until someone comes up behind me. We only have a handful of parking spaces by the doctor's spot at the side door, and my co-workers usually take those before I get there. I park in the patient parking nearest the side door, and sometimes noisy protestors are up on the hill with a megaphone preaching, or trying to talk over the fence to anyone entering the facility. I have to squeeze by the prickly bushes to enter the door.

Once I'm inside, I turn off the alarm if I'm the first one in, go up front to clock in, and make sure everything is in its place for the day. I've been working there so long that I know most everything that goes on, and I can fill in to help almost wherever needed. First I get all the paperwork for the procedures arranged on clipboards so we're ready for the patients. I'm the sterilization tech and assist the nurse, so it's my job to make sure the rooms are clean and ready and the doctor has all his sterilized instruments. Before that, though, I put my earbuds in and start my gospel music to keep me calm for the day.

One of my primary job duties is to weigh the suctioned fetal material to make sure the abortion doctor has completely evacuated the woman's uterus. I'm also responsible to make sure all the rooms are set up with speculums and drape sheets. But I don't set up the procedure room unless I know for sure the woman will actually go through with it, because sometimes they decide to take the pill instead or choose not to have the procedure done after all. When we're short-handed or really busy, I'll help out up front because I'm trained to help out in most of the duties. But otherwise I hang out back in my corner, which is in the autoclave room. Everyone else is full time, but I'm usually gone by midafternoon, depending on the number of surgeries we have.

Entering the Facility

When patients first walk in the door they're in a little breeze-way with just a bulletin board on the left. It has brochures for different types of birth control. Then they come into another door on the right into the waiting area with the lobby. There we can see everyone who walks in, and we greet them and ask the reason for their visit; we have them sign in and mark why they've come. Then we immediately take their name off the slip so nobody else can see their name or what they're there for.

It's a very bright atmosphere. We have the blinds open, so sunlight is coming in; the lights are bright, and we have light-colored wallpaper. The television is always on; it used to be turned to the food channel, but everyone complained about it, especially the ones that hadn't had anything to eat since 12 o'clock last night, so then we tried CNN and they didn't like that one, so it's on soap operas now.

The chairs are blue and burgundy, and I have them color-coordinated, so you have one blue chair, then one burgundy, around the walls of the waiting room. There are plants in the center of the room on the coffee table. There's a bathroom they can use; the T.V. is on the right wall, and there's a brochure wall stand with different types of birth control and adoption information. It smells nice, like fresh linen-scented disinfectant.

Procedures Before the Abortion Takes Place

When the patients start arriving, they sign in and check which reason they are here: gynecological or birth control office visit, to take the abortion pill, to have a surgical abortion procedure, or a follow-up appointment.

The patients must by South Carolina law fill out an online form 24 hours in advance; they can print it out themselves or take a screen shot, and they email it to us so we can print it out for their file. Then we need to see their identification, but not everyone has one. We can't do anything if they don't have some school or state I.D. Some drive themselves to the clinic, and we ask them how they got there and where their license is. They say, "I am who I am." We respond, "Well, you should have proof." They may present their Social Security card, but we can't take it because it doesn't have their photo on it. One tried to say, "I have my daughter's Social Security card." But we told her since it wasn't hers and didn't have her photo, we couldn't use it. We don't even need their Social Security card.

The biggest issue for identification is with the underage patients. They have to have the long form birth certificate because it has both the father's and mother's names, and the child's legal name. Our law requires children 16 and under to have parental consent. If they are 17 and over, they don't need it. They have to have one parent present to sign, but their other parent has to be named.

First the women take a pregnancy test to make sure they are indeed pregnant. At that point, we collect the money for the ultrasound and possibly the abortion also, if they're abortion-minded. The ultrasound is next, to see how far along their pregnancy has progressed; standard procedure is to ask them if they want to watch the ultrasound. One technician is trained specifically for ultrasounds, but sometimes the doctor performs them if they are questionable. If they are very borderline over the date or too early, we can't do anything. We have to see a sac in the uterus because it could be in the tube still. In that case, we send them to a lab to do a blood pregnancy test. And then they have to come back at a later date, but they don't get charged for another ultrasound.

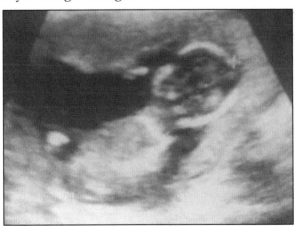

After signing paperwork, by law they have to wait an hour, so that's when they get their blood test via finger stick to see their hemoglobin levels; we also get their vitals to make sure they're healthy enough to go through with an abortion of either type.

Usually they've read the website and have already decided to have the pill or surgery when they come to the clinic.

The Abortion Pill

The pill, or "medical abortion," has become more and more popular over the years. The "abortion pill" is actually a set of pills called RU-486, and it costs $595 at our clinic. The first day, the woman takes a pill called mifepristone. This basically blocks the living fetus from receiving much-needed progesterone to live. One to two days later, she takes a set of four pills of misoprostol, which causes her body to cramp and expel the dead remains.[33]

If they're too far along for the pill, past 10 weeks, they might decide to keep the baby after all or go ahead and choose the surgery. The surgery can be done 12 weeks from conception, which equals around 14 weeks' gestational age; it costs $695.

After waiting an hour, they take their one pill at the clinic, or sometimes they leave to take it at home. Sometimes people bring them back and don't even use them. They get a refund if they don't take it. They also get a refund if taking the pill doesn't work, but they can decide to have the surgery if they choose to do so, without paying the extra cost.

They leave with a prescription for pain meds and their instructions. Then, 24 or 48 hours later, they can take the second set of four pills. Then they are instructed to come back two weeks after the pill or three weeks after the surgical procedure to determine that the pregnancy was evacuated successfully. They have an ultra-sound, performed by the doctor.

Surgical Abortion Without General Anesthesia:

Those who either can't or don't want the pill choose the surgery, usually with general anesthesia. We don't get many that choose the local anesthesia—usually they take it like a champ, but occasionally one or two will scream, curse, or cry hysterically.

One day, Anna[1] came in and said, "I read about it online and I think I want to have the surgical abortion, but I'd rather not have the anesthesia that puts you out."

I said, "Listen, are you really sure? Even though he's numbing the cervix, you'll feel everything inside. So it'll be like the first stages of labor. You'll feel it like cramps as if you were having labor pains. It doesn't cost any extra to have the anesthesia."

Tears streaming down her face, she said, "I've decided I'm going to do it without the anesthesia."

So I gave her the proper paperwork, saying, "Here's your paperwork for the surgical abortion. Sit down here to fill it out and just wait for us to call you back up." A while later, after she finished it, I called her to come and said, "Now I need you to sign this other piece of paperwork that goes to the lab; then you can go to the bathroom for a urine sample. Bring the sample out with you and take it to the nurse in the lab room right here by the bathroom. The nurse will process it to make sure the test shows two lines, which means you're pregnant."

After Anna came out of the bathroom, I said, "Okay, now you can wait in the back waiting area down that hall until we're ready for you to come and pay." We don't do insurance, so everyone has to pay beforehand for their services. When it was Anna's turn, the office manager said, "Okay, that will be $695 for the surgical abortion. Are you paying cash or credit?" Anna paid with a credit card, and then she was told, "Now you can go back to the waiting room until it's time for your ultrasound."

The ultrasound tech called for Anna and said, "Hi, my name is Molly; you can come with me for your vaginal ultrasound now." She took her into that room and said, "Now I need you to undress from the waist down, and I'll be back in a minute."

I don't have anything to do with the ultrasound procedures, but the tech performed the ultrasound then and asked her, as always, "Do you want to watch the ultrasound?" Half of the women typically say no, but Anna decided to watch it. The tech said, "You're eight weeks along. And we did this at 10:10, so now by state

---

[1] Anna is a fictional patient

law you have to wait an hour until 11:10 to come back for the procedure. You can sit in the building or go back out to the car. Just be back by 11:10 if you drive anywhere."

"Okay," Anna replied, "I'll just hang out here in the waiting room."

Sometimes people leave at that point and don't come back until the next day, because they don't read the website right that they have to wait 24 hours, so they only have lab and ultrasound done the first day, and then come back the next day for the actual abortion procedure.

After the ultrasound, during that hour of waiting, we had Anna go to the lab to get her temperature and blood pressure checked, along with a finger prick to test her hemoglobin level. Hers was fine, but sometimes if it's too low, we'll start an IV bag of fluids to see if that will help the hemoglobin. Sometimes all it is, is that their fluids are low, and they just need some fluids. Again, we told her that doing this procedure without anesthesia would be extremely uncomfortable, but she didn't change her mind. Personally, I think some people like Anna feel they need to be punished, and that's why they go with just the local.

When Anna's hour was up, one of us called her name and asked for her date of birth and last name to make sure we had the right person. We sent her to the counseling room, where she spoke with the doctor. He asked, "Are you sure this is something you really want to do?"

She answered fretfully, "This has been such a hard decision, you know? I'm a Christian, and I don't believe in this, but the timing is just horrible for me to be pregnant, and the guy is not supportive. I would never do this under normal circumstances."

He responded, "All right, then, we will go ahead and get you ready."

I directed Anna to the bathroom again and said, "Make sure your bladder is completely empty." When she was finished, I took her to the procedure room and said, "I need you to get undressed from the waist down and have a seat on the blue pad on the table. Then open the white sheet up and lay it across you. We'll come back for you after we're done with our other patients in front of you."

Later, the doctor and I came in, and he asked her again, "Are you comfortable with your decision to go through with this, and are you sure you don't want to go to sleep? I'm going to numb your cervix, but you'll feel everything happening on the inside. It will be like the first stages of labor, very uncomfortable contractions."

Very quietly, a tear-stained Anna answered, "Yes, I've made my decision, even though it's something I don't believe in, but I need to do it."

"Okay," he said, "then put your feet in the stirrups and scoot down to the edge of the bed."

I had already set the sterile table up, ready for the doctor to use, so I rechecked her blood pressure before he started.

With clean, gloved hands, he cleaned her pubic area with hydrogen peroxide and then inserted the speculum to open up her cervix. Next, he washed her vagina with hydrogen peroxide inside and out. He said, "You're going to feel a sharp pinch now." He used a long, skinny needle to numb the opening of her cervix with injected lidocaine. Then he started the dilation process. The dilators are sterling silver, and he used the smallest instrument first, then the next size up and so on, one right after the other, up to size eight.

During this whole process, some women are very talkative, usually talking about nothing, just to keep their minds off what's going on. They want me to talk with them, and Anna was no exception. I said, "I'm not a talkative person, but if you start the conversation I will participate." Then she started talking, like they do, about what led her there and why she decided to do this.

Anna said to me, "I normally would never do anything like this because my family has never believed abortion is right, but I just don't like the guy who's the father. I thought he would be somebody special, and he turned out to be a bum. He said he loved me and he would be there for me no matter what, but in the end, it was just a one-night stand. After that night he revealed his true colors and was an absolute jerk. He's actually still married and has two kids with her. When I found out I was pregnant and told him, he told me to have the abortion because he didn't want to commit or help out in any way."

I responded, "Yeah, a lot of women come here for those reasons." As we continued our idle chatter, I handed the doctor the size 12 curette. Then he connected it to the suction machine and turned it on. The tubing is so opaque all we could see was the blood going through it for five or so minutes until it was finished. It made its loud humming sound, which is somewhat quieter than a vacuum cleaner.

It was over quite quickly, in a matter of a few minutes, and Anna couldn't see the suctioning happening; she just saw me and the tray table of instruments positioned next to her.

She said, "How much longer is this going to take? It hurts."

The doctor, seated, replied, "I'm done now," as he turned off the machine.

While he was talking to her, I gathered the dirty instruments, the used tubing, and the jar of specimen. I took it all out of the room so it would be gone before she got off the table. We don't leave patients alone at that point, so he stayed in the room with her until I returned. I started the blood pressure cuff again. We checked her vitals, and I said, "Okay, now the doctor is going to do a second vaginal ultrasound to make sure the uterus is empty." He also checked to make sure she wasn't forming any blood clots. Some women have a tipped uterus, so blood will form there.

He said to her, "Everything is okay, and I'm going to look under the microscope to make sure I got it all out."

I brought in our wheelchair, which is like a recliner on wheels. "Your blood pressure is 118 over 78," I reported. I took the blood pressure cuff off and got her to sit up. "You don't feel dizzy, do you?"

"No," she replied, "I feel fine." Her tears had completely dried by now. I helped her scoot off the bed and transferred her to the chair.

"Now I'm going to put up the footrest and recline you," I warned. After that, I rolled her over to the recovery room. We never put more than two people at a time in that room so they have privacy. I said, "In 20-30 minutes, the nurse will come to check your vitals again and take you to the bathroom to make sure you're not bleeding heavily or passing any clots."

Her nurse, Connie, took care of her, let her get dressed, and reviewed her post-care instructions. Connie informed her, "You can have some pain pills now if you want, and we have water, sodas, or juice if you like." We keep regular nonprescription Tylenol or Ibuprofen, just like what women would take for regular menstrual pain.

The nurse walked her out to make sure she had a ride, but there was no one there for her.

Anna said, "I'll just wait right here. My sister's on her way," gesturing to the front waiting area.

The nurse said, "No, come on back to the waiting room."

"Why can't I wait right here?" asked Anna.

"Because we have to walk you to the door to make sure you have someone with you," Connie answered.

A few minutes later, Anna announced, "Okay, my sister's outside now."

Connie walked her to the door and said, "Good-bye," and Anna's experience at our clinic was over in around three hours—at least until she came back for her three-week check-up, or another abortion, or other gynecological services.

Abortion with General Anesthesia

When a woman has the surgery under general anesthesia, the procedure is slightly different. After taking her to the bathroom and the procedure room, I say, "The nurse will be in to start your IV in a minute." The woman doesn't get put out with her medication until the doctor comes in and talks to her again. Then I don't go in until after the IV is started. I have to hold her legs straight during the procedure so they don't flop and so her feet don't come out of the stirrups. The nurse stays in the room the whole time also.

When the procedure is finished we all have to slide her back up on the table and transfer her to the recliner. She comes awake in the recovery room, often asking, "How did I get over here?" "Did I get up and not know it?"

Specimen Examination

Now, it's my job to go take care of the jar of specimen. The specimen is in a "sock" that I take out of the jar to put on the petri dish to weigh it. With the naked eye, the earlier ones mostly just look like bloody tissue at that point. Sometimes at nine weeks you can begin to see more detail still intact. Then I open the sock and empty the contents into a second petri dish for the doctor to examine in the lab under the microscope to make sure fetal tissue is present. He places that petri dish in a box to carry to another room, where he takes it out of the box and dumps it into a medical waste bucket to eventually be incinerated. The medical waste bucket has a red liner. After the waste disposal man does his pickup every other week, I sterilize the container and put in another red bag. We keep it frozen so it doesn't smell.

One time I weighed a specimen and the weight was lower than it should have been, so I told the doctor, "I think you need to re-ultrasound her because her weight doesn't match up to how far along she was." He hadn't done the second ultrasound yet, so he went back in to finish the job.

He looks at the early ones under the microscope, but if they are larger, like 10-12 weeks along, he told me he can verify on the ultrasound that he took everything out. Anything less than 46 grams, which is usually up to 8-9 weeks, he looks under the microscope to make sure he has all the pieces.

In the past I was very curious what those pieces looked like put back together. It wasn't a job requirement, but I was interested to see it. The younger specimens were not so well-developed, and they don't have very distinguishable body parts after having gone through the suction tube. But when they're 10-12 weeks old, the head, spine, and extremities, although fragile, are more clearly formed. Sometimes, I would call the nurse to come look at them with me. But after doing it a few times, I didn't think it was necessary anymore. There was no point. Now, it bothers me a little. I just don't look in the sack anymore. It does bother me, especially when they're more developed. Sometimes when they're further along, the nurse might still ask me, "Are we going to look at that one?"

I tell her, "No, we are not."

A few minutes later she'll ask again, "Dionne, where's the sack?"

"I told you, we're not looking at it. I've already put it up."

Sometimes the women ask, "Can I take the remains home to bury?"

I reply, "Well, if it's all right with the doctor, I don't mind putting it in something for you."

I think only one has ever followed through and taken it home with her; typically the response after seeing it on the petri dish is something like, "That's it? Well, shit, I pass more than that when I'm on my period."

I say, "Well, you wanted to see it; I'm showing it to you."

Stories from Inside

There's so much that goes on inside the clinic that is crazy. A lot of people think the doctors are heartless and don't care about the patients. I wish I could really sit down and tell them that the doctors are not as heartless as people think they are. They turn away a lot of women who don't have their minds made up, or women who come in rude or disrespectful. Then the doctors are irritated, so we tell the women they need to go elsewhere. They say, "No, I'm going to be good." By then it's too late, but they think because they're flashing some money around that the doctors are going to be okay with their rudeness, that at the end of the day it's about the dollars. But that's not true. The doctors have our backs. They don't let patients disrespect us or them, telling the women, "You can go somewhere else." Some women come for only birth control or their pap smears and yearly physicals, but they've never had an abortion that we know of.

A lot of the ladies get upset with us because they have to wait so long in the office. They think they have to wait too long to have the procedure or take the pill, when they could just come in, fill out their paperwork, and go home. Half of them don't even want to have the ultrasound done, and usually it's because they already know they're too far for us. But they cop an attitude with us because there's nothing we can do. Sometimes they wig out while they're on the table. One woman started acting insane and pulled out all her IV's. Out of patience, Dr. One said, "I'm going to talk to her. She can either do the pill or come back on Dr. Two's week."

Sometimes women are on drugs and don't tell us. We had one girl come in and I knew she had taken something; I just didn't know what. She freaked out. Luckily enough, we were done with the procedure and she was coming off of the propofol. As she woke up, this woman just forgot where she was, and she freaked. She seemed to be having an argument with a female, so I'm guessing she must have been fighting with this girl before she got there or the day before, because she picked up where she left off. She was cussing and fussing and trying to fight, and we had to hold her down and try to get her totally awake so she could know where she was. Finally when she did, and she looked around, she said, "What's going on? Did I say something?"

"Oh yeah," I responded. "You called us all kind of names and tried to fight us."

She apologized. "I'm so sorry, I thought you was somebody else."

We told her, "The propofol has a different reaction on everybody. It makes some people cry, it makes some people laugh, it makes some very talkative." I was thinking to myself, *it makes you combative if you're on something and not telling us about it beforehand.*

Some of the women come back over and over, up to ten times. For all we know, they've gone to other abortion clinics, too. We act like a patient is new unless she complains about having to go through all the steps, such as, the blood testing. You get some that say, "That's going to hurt."

The nurse, irritated, retorts, "You've been here before and you know it's not that bad—it's just a finger prick."

Once a woman asked me, "Do you enjoy working here?"
"Well, it's a job. What do you do for a living?"
"Stripper."
"Really?" I said, "Do you enjoy it?"
"Yeah," she answered, "it pays real good."

I do believe in a woman's choice, even though I think the women having abortions are making the wrong choice. I'm glad they have a safe environment to come to at our clinic, because otherwise they'd find an unhealthy place to have it done.

We do a lot of abortions. I did some numbers; it's wild, but in my clinic alone, the race that has the most abortions is the Hispanic race, and then African Americans, Caucasians, and Asians. Sometimes I feel totally sorry for some of the ones that come in there, especially the Hispanic women, because some of them don't speak English. They can't even read and write, so that lets you know they're not educated; they don't know their options, that there are other options out there. I don't speak Spanish, so I don't know how those conversations go in the clinic. I could try to talk to any of them and explain to them that there are better options, but it's complicated. For instance, some Asian women would rather sit back and let a man talk for them, and that really ticks me off. But it's not my place to say anything, and I'm not there to judge.

We do get certain other women that have the men talk for them. They just sit there and nod. I want to shout, "Open up your mouth!" But they're scared to, because they have to go home to this man. You just can't imagine the stories that some women tell us. They don't necessarily have to listen to that man that they supposedly "love," because if he truly loved her he wouldn't be bringing her to an abortion clinic. That's my opinion.

Teen Abortions

A parent's supposed to love a child unconditionally, not force her to make a decision to give up her child. Nobody forced them to give up theirs, so why are the parents forcing their children to give up theirs? That I don't understand, because it's our job as parents to help our children in any way possible. I told my kids, "I'm there for you 100 percent," even when my son told me that his girlfriend was pregnant and having his baby. I was surprised at first, but I wanted him to know I support him in life.

If they're 17 or older, by South Carolina law they don't need parental consent to have an abortion, and their parents don't even know they're doing it. But I do believe that we would have a lot fewer abortions if some of these kids were taught at home about their options. We get a lot of kids that aren't educated. Some of them are grown women but they're not educated. They've never been told that you can go up the road to the OB clinic and get on Medicaid; you can get help, and before the baby even gets here you can get on housing. There's a lot of help out there for women, but they've got to know, and if they don't know or if they're not being told that there are other options, they end up calling our clinic.

They just have to be educated, and I believe that it should start in the homes, but a lot of parents don't feel comfortable talking to their kids about sex or their options if they did get pregnant. No, they just talk some about disease, and yes, there are diseases out there, but that's not the only thing they need to worry about. There's teen pregnancy, and then you get people getting raped, and the consequences of that. These days and times, when a female finds out she's pregnant, the first thing she asks, "What's the number for the abortion clinic?" I want to say, "No, that shouldn't be the first thought that comes into your mind when you find out you're pregnant. That's a life, a precious gift that has been given to you." And to throw it away—I just don't understand it, but that's their decision, not mine.

One day a mother walked in with her very young teenage daughter, Mia.[2] She said, "She's here for the pill. We read your website, and we'd like to get this taken care of today."

Lorena at the front desk asked, "Have you read all the information we had on there? Did you print the proof and bring it with you?

Mia's mother said, "Yes, here it is," and proceeded to turn in the 24-hour consent form.

Lorena handed her the forms she needed to fill out and instructed them to take a seat in the waiting area. She said, "Please fill out all these. We'll need ID's from both of you and her long-form birth certificate.

Her mother scanned the paperwork and asked, "Why do you need her father's name on this? He's not in her life and doesn't even know she got pregnant."

Lorena said, "That's what we're required to get from every minor."

DHEC has a lot of details we have to ask the girls and report on. Some girls ask, "Why do you need to know if I've finished school or not?" It's not for us—we don't care, but DHEC needs that information.

Once the paperwork is filled out, I take the daughter to get her urine sample, to make sure we get a positive pregnancy test. Next they see Kelly to collect the payment; once that is received, she also has to have an ultrasound. We inform them it's an hour wait, and during that time we get her lab work done. When the hour's up, we call the parent(s) and child back into a private room with the doctor; he talks to them alone, counsels them, and then retrieves the pills to give them. He makes sure during this time that she's not being forced and that it's something she wants to have done. We have Spanish speakers to translate if necessary.

Sometimes the parents think that we can't tell their small, young teenage daughter is farther along in the pregnancy than they told us, but the ultrasound doesn't lie. We do not perform the abortions if they are one day past the legal limit of 12 weeks, and the

---

[2] Mia is a fictional patient.

fetus is going to be a certain size by that time, no matter the size, age, or race of the girl. Plenty of folks have gotten mad at us and left, sometimes to go to another clinic that does later abortions.

Why I Continue to Work There

Deep down, I'm glad there is a place like the clinic, because, trust and believe, some of the girls who come in there, that don't want these kids, they will find a way to get rid of them, healthy or not. I wish there were no abortion clinics. I wish people would be more thankful about life, but the way things are now, I really don't see that happening. Some folks that do have their children and then later down the line think, "Oh, this is not for me," will end up killing their child anyway. So yes, you should have just aborted if you're going to end up killing the baby when it's two or three or four or five because it doesn't fit into your lifestyle anymore when things get hard. Hell, life is hard. I wish they would give up their children for adoption instead of keeping them in these situations. There are many people who want children and can't have them.

I know it's kind of crazy to say, but I love my job. I love what we offer these people because, believe it or not, some actually feel like they don't have a choice. You can talk to some folks 'til you're blue in the face, but they've got their minds made up—that's what they're going to do, that's why there're there. For others, you can tell that this isn't what they really want. After hearing a reason, a calm voice—just knowing that there's somebody else out there or something else they can do—some take that option and say, "No, I can't do this." And you'd be surprised at the number of women that actually do change their mind. It is a high number. There are a lot who are on the fence, and a little nudge will push them the right way; it usually does, and they have their child. Or maybe they go somewhere else and they don't come back to our clinic, but I like to think that they had the child.

And then you get the ones that want you to tell them what they should do. And I just plain tell them, "Look, I can't tell you what you can and can't do. But if you want my opinion, I can give you that, and I can tell you what I would do. Me, personally, this is something I wouldn't do, because there are options out there. You can get help if you don't have the help of your family. There's help out there. There are organizations that can help you find a home if you need one. So if this is something you don't want to do, then don't do it." And I have had a lot of girls change their minds and end up seeking help. Because there is help out there—they just have to look and ask questions.

———————

We had one girl who had some doubts about going through with the abortion when I checked her in. I told her, "If you aren't sure, then you shouldn't be here." And she said, "No, I believe this is what I want to do." I gave her the paperwork, and she had the ultrasound; she still stayed through the entire waiting time for the pill. She went in when it was time, and then said she didn't want to go through with it. I said, "Okay," and she asked, "You're not mad at me?"

I said, "No, it's your decision. You have the right to decide what to do."

She replied, "But I've wasted your time."

I told her, "No, it's about what you want; if you don't want to, you don't have to." So we gave her back her money. She gave me a hug and she left.

Another woman who changed her mind had waited the whole time to take the pill. She actually went through the counseling with the doctor and everything. He left the room to get the medicine, and shortly after, she opened the door, poked her head out, and said, "I don't think I'm going to be able to do it."

I said, "Okay. I will let him know." And I walked her out.

She told me, "Thank you."

I said, "Let me take you to Kelly, because you need a refund. You get it all back, minus the ultrasound fee of $160."

She said, "Oh yeah, I forgot about that."

When the doctor came back, he asked me, "What happened?"

I said, "She changed her mind, so I took her back to Kelly."

He said, "Oh, okay."

Some women ask me, "Well, what would you do?" And I'm the one who always seems to get that question. When I'm on the phone, I tell them, "You can't base your decision on what I would do, because I wouldn't be calling here in the first place. I mean, if I got pregnant, then it was meant to be. I'm having that baby because I knew the consequences of having sex, so if I got pregnant then this was meant to be and I'm going to have my child. But because that's something I would do, I can't tell you that that's what you should do. But if you are asking me for my opinion, I would have my child, regardless of the situation." I have told a lot of people that. It just depends what they want out of life.

We have quite a few that change their mind and leave; it could be as many as one in four or five. Probably a lot don't even make it inside our doors, but we don't calculate or talk about those no-shows. Because there are so many walk-ins, they make up for the no-shows, and then some.

More Stories from Inside

We get some women that are being forced, but they're not going to say they are, because if they say those words, then we wouldn't be able to accept them as patients. We have to tell them, especially when mothers bring in their young kids, as part of our conversation on the phone: "Well, you can't force her to have it; this is something she has to want to do." When she's in there talking to the doctor, and she says at least one time, "This is something I don't want to do," the doctor's not going to do it, and we're not going to force her to do it. And the mothers and some fathers get mad at us because we won't do those abortions. She doesn't want this done, so no, we're not going to do it until she says this is something she wants to do and that she's comfortable with her decision; otherwise, we can't do her procedure. She can be 13, 12, it doesn't matter: if she says she doesn't want this done, we won't do it. And then we have to take the fallout from the parents or the boyfriend. We say, "Well, it's not about you; it's what she wants, and if she doesn't want it,

62

then we can't do it." The number of people that we actually turn away is pretty high. I was surprised at the number of the people that we've turned away.

We get all types of people that come to the clinic. You get your high-sodiddy[3] folks that want to rent out the entire place so they're the only patients. We get the Bible-thumpers—believe me, we get plenty of those—that holler about, "I don't believe in abortion, but this is something I can't do right now. This is what I need to do; hopefully God'll forgive me, and I hope nobody judges me." We get a lot of those girls. And then you get the ones that seem like they're "off the streets," but they can't be. If they'd been off the streets, they wouldn't have had the money to do this. And we get strippers—oh man! Some of their stories are crazy.

Many times women are too far along and try to bribe us, but we can't do it, so they get mad at us because we can't or won't. It's not something that we do past the limit, but they think that we're supposed to do it because they're paying us. We say, "No, you can take your money and go somewhere else." The clinic's not there to make a buck. Yes, everyone that goes to a job every day, they're concerned about making a dollar. But at the end of the day, believe it or not, we care more about the patient than we do about the mighty dollar. If the patient tells us she's not comfortable, she doesn't think this is what she wants to do, then we tell her, "Don't do it; you've got time. There's a lot of help out there. If this isn't what you want to do, then just don't do it."

Some tell us their life stories. Then, you get the ones that holler about, "I don't think I can do this. It's just too hard raising a child." Now, come on; when my father passed away, my mom had us to raise, and if I do say so myself, she did a damn good job. She worked hard to take care of us, to give us what we needed and some of what we wanted, but mostly what we needed. But she did it. She was a single mother with small children, had just lost her husband, but she stepped up. She never mistreated us, even when we probably needed it sometimes.

---

[3] Slang for "high-society"

So when people holler about, "Oh, I can't do this. I've already got a child," I want to say, "You already know the consequences of having sex. The possibility of you getting pregnant—it's going to happen if you keep having unprotected sex." I think that anybody who is old enough to lie down and have sex is old enough to take care of a child. If not, then you shouldn't be having sex, plain and simple. I told mine, "If you go out there and get pregnant, get a baby, then you're going to have that child and take care of it. Trust and believe I'll help with what I can, but that child is your responsibility. You're going to raise her or him." Luckily enough, my daughter is 26 and she has never had one; my son is 23 and he has a little girl and he's taking care of her. So, for young girls that think they can't do it, there's no such thing. Even if you don't have your family's support, there's support out there. You just have to be willing to do the work and ask questions. Because if you ask questions, people will answer and help.

Sometimes you can hear our "frequent fliers" in the waiting room interacting with the "newbies." They tell them, "You should do the pill; it's not as painful as everybody says."

Then you get these women that figure abortion is their birth control. Instead of taking something or doing something, they'd rather come in here and have an abortion. You get the ones that think, "Well, I'm not really having an abortion, I'm taking a pill." I want to say, "You're having an abortion, not a miscarriage." They're forcing a miscarriage, so they are aborting, but they've got it in their minds that they're not. But it's surprising how some people think the pill is not killing their baby when it actually is. I guess it helps them sleep at night to think, *Well, I'm just having a miscarriage.* No, you're forcing it—it's the same as having the suction done. It's just a mind thing.

For some reason, if some women find out they're too far along to take the pill, their whole attitude changes. They say, "No, if I could do the pill I would, but if I can't do the pill, then I'm not going to have the surgery done." We let them know, "Okay, then, that's your decision."

Some of them ask, "Which is better, the pill or the surgery?" Neither one is better. It's all about your preference. The pill is a two-step method; the procedure is done in one day, so it's over with. It just depends on what you want. It's different for every girl. Some afterwards can be a little emotional, and some will talk your head off, cheering, cracking jokes, talking and wanting to know when they can have sex again, or when they can have a drink.

Everybody's different. The ones that are emotional are the ones that were on the fence. They weren't quite sure that this is something they wanted to do, because it wasn't the right time for them. They are a little emotional after, but by the time they leave, it's like nothing happened. They were emotional for that minute, and then they're back to who they were, talking about going out, when can they drink and have sex and all that. Believe it or not, the main question all of them have is, "When can I have sex again?" We tell them, "You have to wait three weeks," and, oh man, it's like a burden. "Really? Why I gotta wait that long?" We tell them, "Because you can get an infection. Hello!" Some do wait, and some don't. Because we've actually had a lot that come back in for their three-week follow-up and they're pregnant again. It's just wild.

Occasionally people are obviously on drugs. We had a girl clearly high, smelling so badly of weed that we told her she had to wash her clothes and come back a different day. I don't know if she smoked it in her car right before she came in, but the smell was so strong we had to spray down the waiting area when she left.

One lady tried to convince us she didn't know how she could be pregnant, because she hadn't had sex. The doctor told her, "I only know of one lady who became pregnant as a virgin, and that was Mary, and your name isn't Mary."

When people find out they're pregnant with twins, it's a whole different story. Often, that discovery alone will change their minds, and they keep the babies. It's surprising that's what changes their minds. Like, it's okay to end the life of one baby but not two. One time there was a couple that had twins and wanted us to abort just one of them. We told them it didn't work that way. That wasn't an option, sorry. That just wasn't something we could do for them.

Sad to say, we have "frequent fliers." We have a lot who come repeatedly. I've known women to have up to ten surgical abortions and up to eight times taking the pill. There's no limit to how many they can have, and some do it multiple times in one year. There are other clinics within driving distance, so there's no telling how many they have actually had in total. One came in so often, I asked her if she ever used the birth control we prescribed to her. She said she had given it to someone else to use because she refused to take it. I said, "But you've been in here multiple times." She said, "It's all good." I replied, "This is not good for your body, but it's whatever you want to do." She said she didn't want to take any birth control but loved to have sex.

The [pro-life] protestors outside can be brutal to some of the ladies that come in. Some of the women coming in here really don't have any choice. This is the last place they wanted to come, because some of them do want their child. For example, one of the ladies that came in was going through fertility treatments, and her baby ended up dying. She had to come in to have a D&C, and she was harassed by those weekend people. This lady was in tears because she wanted her child. They don't know the situation that some of those girls are in. Some of them can be a little understanding, but others can be cruel. I just wish that they would be a little less aggressive, like the [sidewalk counselor] ladies during the week, but I guess you can't pick and choose who's going to be out there.

Follow-up Visit

The women must come back for an office visit to make sure there's nothing left in the uterus to cause an infection. This happens two weeks after the pill or three weeks after the surgery. It consists of the doctor performing a vaginal examination and an ultrasound, and that visit is included in the initial price.

When the women come back in for their post-abortive check-ups, they don't ever tell us their emotions regarding the abortion. A few say, "You won't see me again," but we do. Once a lady came back, and I tried to act like I didn't know who she was. She said, "I told you I wasn't coming back, but I'm here again. You don't remember me?"

I replied, "Well, no, but the name looks familiar."

When women take the pill to have an abortion, we tell them they can get pregnant soon after taking it. Seems like half of them don't believe us, so they come back in there, thinking that they can convince us it's the same pregnancy. But we have the ultrasound and can see it's not the same pregnancy, that they should be farther along than they are. It just doesn't work like that.

The abortion pill doesn't always terminate the pregnancy. In that case, we offer them a choice of a refund or the surgical procedure at no additional cost. If the pill fails to do its job, some say it's a sign to have the baby, and they end up keeping it after all. One woman did the pill with all the steps, but the pregnancy was progressing still, so she chose to keep the baby. She brought her baby in to show us. The baby was really cute and we were so happy to see it. It was in the afternoon with no other patients around. Normally we don't allow babies or children to come in at all. We get a lot of people who want to bring their kids in, so I tell them they can come back in the afternoon when we aren't doing abortions.

7

Volunteering Outside the

Abortion Clinic

Shiela waiting at the driveway

Shiela writing:

As I mentioned, in August 2018, I took training in Green-ville, S.C., to serve locally outside our abortion clinic. The approach I was taught is to be prayerful and peaceful, and absolutely law-abiding at all times. We always go with a partner, so even though I was terrified at first, I went right out that next week with Carrie, and I haven't looked back since.

Although I'm a redhead and extra sensitive to the sun and varying temperatures, God has given me a special grace to be able to handle being outside during this ministry. It's really the only time I generally spend out of doors. I dress appropriately for the day, prepare to bring all of my life-affirming literature, signs and gifts, and then pray that morning for God to speak through me. What if I am the only friendly face these people encounter during the day? I need to portray the heart of Jesus, because I believe He would have spent time outside an abortion clinic; He would have been healing and forgiving women of their guilt and condemnation, then telling them to leave that place and go love their children.

The following are prayers I often pray outside the clinic:

God, use me to bless others today, and let babies be saved, and their parents spared from committing this atrocity. God, let them feel your divine, perfect love; Jesus, appear to them so they flee that clinic; Holy Spirit, convict them to do what is right and know it is wrong to take the life of their child. Jesus, let them see you through my smile. Speak through me and give me the words to say to convince them to choose life and leave as happy parents. Change the hearts of the employees so they realize that abortion is an evil that they don't want to participate in anymore. Let people see the light of Jesus shine through my face when I smile at them. Let my presence on the sidewalk make a difference. You've specifically called and triple-anointed me for this ministry, so use me mightily. Angels in the heavenly realm, be released into this atmosphere. May this place be shut down in Jesus' name!

My fellow pro-life advocates and I have discussed more than once how this is not an easy ministry, and it's definitely not glamorous. Week after week, for hours at a time, we stand outside our city's abortion clinic in the direct and humid summer heat praying for cloud cover as the thermometer reaches the 90s. We're thankful to be living in the South during the winter cold; although the mornings can occasionally get into the 20s, generally they stay in the 30s and 40s. Then there are the rainy deluges, and even storms from hurricanes, in between. (Fortunately I've only ever had to leave once from a thunderstorm, because usually they occur overnight.) We often lament that the spring and fall here are much too short, but we are grateful for moderately pleasant days when they occur.

The abortion clinic is on a very busy two-lane county road between an interstate and the downtown hospital system, but the actual building sits hidden mostly behind a hill and is surrounded by the tall, brown picket fence shown on the cover of this book. The driveway leading to the only opening in the fence is about twenty feet long and fifteen feet wide, just enough for two cars to pass each other. Although there isn't a physical sidewalk, we are allowed to congregate in the dirt on either side of the driveway, because it's all publicly accessible up to the fence line.

We literally only have a couple of seconds to attract someone's attention to see if they want to stop to talk to us on the driveway. They have been told by clinic workers not to stop for us, though, so we are most often ignored. I wave and have a clipboard with a smiley face that says, "Hi, can I help you?" If they do stop, we often have mere seconds to speak with them on the driveway before someone else drives up behind them. Whenever another car approaches, we have to quickly jump back so we're not blocking any traffic that's trying to turn in from the busy street or come out of the clinic. We have to remain above reproach so there's no reason for the abortion doctors to report us to the police. They have a security camera trained on us at all times. That might seem to be nerve wracking, but it has come in helpful when counter-protesters are on-site, and the police need to view what has been taking place.

Many people driving in ask if I work there. I say, "No, I'm not with the abortion clinic or the pregnancy resource center (PRC). I volunteer outside to let women know about their options." At that point, they typically roll their window up and quickly speed up to drive into the abortion clinic parking lot.

Very often, people will yell expletives as they drive by or drive in. We also hear, "God hates you!" "Women against women!" "You should just go home!" Or, "Get a job! Don't you have something better to do? How dare you?"

Although I don't come up to someone's car unless they stop and roll down their window, sometimes people think what we're doing is illegal. We might hear, "Get away or I'll call the police!" Or, "Get the hell away from my car!" as they video us with their phones. Many times people drive by slowly so they can take photos or videos of us. Although I haven't been witness to it, guns have been brandished or pointed towards my fellow advocates.

I always follow the safety guideline of never being alone on the sidewalk. That takes some coordination and planning; thankfully, each year brings more and more volunteers outside to join us. When I first started, only one or two people were dedicated per weekday morning, but now it's common to have four or more. Not every day was covered at first, but that trend has changed. Saturdays have always been busy, since more people are off work then. We did have a temporary setback with the pandemic scare, but a core group remained even then, and overall it has mushroomed substantially.

The Importance of Signage and Attitude

Be humble when you are trying to teach those who are mixed up concerning the truth. For if you talk meekly and courteously to them they are more likely, with God's help, to turn away from their wrong ideas and believe what is true. Then they will come to their senses and escape from Satan's trap of slavery to sin which he uses to catch them whenever he likes, and then they can begin doing the will of God.

2 Timothy 2:25-26

Let us outdo each other in being helpful and kind to each other and in doing good.

Hebrews 10:24

Not everyone who comes out to the "sidewalk" is with the same ministry, but we all have the same goal of saving babies. There are different approaches and attitudes, which can spark some conflict. Although I do believe there are times graphic signage of aborted fetuses can be useful and informative, it is not very conducive to getting the women driving in to stop and talk. People have a right to use whatever signage they would like, but we have occasionally politely requested them to stand more at a distance while we're trying to talk to the people driving inside. While a sign like "GREENVILLE'S DEATH CAMP" may contain truth, it may also come across as harsh to those driving in, and make it more likely for them to pass me by.

Signs are important. At a single glance, they convey a message to the viewer. That message can be eye-catching, shocking, condemning, loving, or life-affirming. In years past, it was normal for pro-lifers to use graphic photos portraying a 12-plus week-old dismembered baby to display the after-effects of surgical abortion. Those types of signage have changed women's minds and resulted in saved babies over the years. Graphic signage is especially helpful, say, at a college campus to educate young adults, so they see the horrors and realities of abortion that perhaps they never knew. To see a dismembered fetus definitely makes the notion of abortion more realistic and not just a vague concept.

Many people, however, are angered or disgusted to see those graphics, and their minds shut off to our message of hope and salvation. We've noticed that more women are willing to stop to talk if those bloody, graphic signs are not used. Although it's true that some people will react well to a strongly worded sign like "Abortion is Murder," many others will be catapulted away from us even more quickly, straight into that clinic to have the abortion; often they associate those types of signs with screaming pro-lifers.

At the driveway I use signs with loving messages about helping and educating women. Our desire is that women/couples stop to talk to us and hopefully change their minds. They need to see us as safe people that they feel they can talk with one-on-one. They are less likely to stop to talk if our message is outwardly negative and condemning and they think we will scream at them that they're going to hell for their actions. We try to love and educate with our signs, displaying "ABORTION PILL REVERSAL .COM" and "Love4You.Life," which is the website for our local informative brochures.

His kindness is meant to lead you to repentance.
Romans 2:4

Jack has been a pro-lifer for decades and is currently associated with Love Life America.[34] He has spoken with a multitude of women and couples who have changed their minds over the years and has a very loving approach to all he encounters. At times he stands by the driveway, and other times he actually climbs up the hill with scaffolding to preach with a speaker over the fence to the people in the parking lot; sometimes he plays worship music. He tries to mentor other, younger men who come out with a passion for the Gospel and the pro-life ministry. I asked him to explain his heart for these women and how he reaches out to them:

If you're out there shouting, "Murderer, murderer!" the chances of winning that person over are slim to none. And if you're beating them over the head with the Gospel, that's not going to work either. You can present the Gospel in such a way as to turn people off completely instead of on. We don't want to do that; we want to bring people the truth as something that's attractive without watering it down. There's a balance. The measure is to see how effective your approach is. Somebody had told me their main goal outside the clinic was to bring people to a saving knowledge of God, so I asked, "How many salvations have you had?" That person had had none, and I said, "So, maybe you ought to change your approach." Something is wrong if you're not successful.

But some of the truths of the Gospel are confrontational. You have to keep in mind what your goal is—your goal is to win them. If you see that you're just aggravating them, then you need to change your tactics. You can be like Paul, all things to all people; we try to embrace people and identify with them, whatever their circumstances. Some people object to us bringing the Gospel in at all, but if you don't, then you're just presenting a humanistic point of view where there are no absolutes and you do things that are right in your own eyes. Really, once they get through the driveway, we're appealing to them with logic and their emotions, also, not make an emotional decision.

Even from a humanistic point of view, it's a baby, a developing baby human, so you will be taking the life of another human. This is truth, even that we're all created in God's image and He even designed that womb to be a safe place, to protect that child in its development. He said, "I formed you even before you were in the womb,"[4] so it's bringing a combination of truth plus the Gospel to it. The science says that life begins at conception, and it's a moral, spiritual issue, not a legal issue—are you prepared to take the life of your own child? God says don't take the life of another, so are you willing to kill your own child? You can't really sugarcoat that; there's just no way to, so it can be confrontational. Maybe it's a way to wake somebody up— this is the truth and am I willing to live with it? The problem with living with it is that abortion is surrounded in shame, secrecy, guilt, and regret. So some carry that for the rest of their lives unless they get counseling; some go off the deep end with drugs, alcohol, and abusive relationships, because that's what they feel they deserve. When they are truthful and lay it down, they are set free. We are for these women— hate the sin, love the sinner. You don't win people with anger. When you're trying to win people over, anger is not the answer—love is.

We're so blessed to have a majority of pro-lifers who have sweet, tender hearts towards all the people driving in. Occasionally, some won't be reflecting the love of Jesus, and I try to gently guide them to my viewpoint, which is, "No matter our sins, God loves everyone as much as He loves you or me." That is a difficult concept to grasp when you're coming face-to-face with an abortionist, I must admit. But if Jesus was willing to die for that man, shouldn't I at least reflect Him? My goal outside the clinic is to shine a light in a dark place. My heart is that people see there is hope, and that life is always the right choice, a better choice for them. If they have already lost a child to abortion, I love them regardless of the decision they've made. I try to find out what's going on with them first and meet them where they're at with love. Some pro-lifers aren't so soft in their approach.

---

[4] Jeremiah 1:5

This is what my friend Nancy had to say on the subject:

I've been witness to a situation that gravely concerns me: people "preaching at" women and men going into an abortion clinic, telling them to repent and asking everyone entering or exiting, "Are you going to kill your baby?" or, "Did you kill your baby?"

I grew up in church and was taught a loving Gospel message from the Bible; however, I recognized a double-standard when I did not see Christians in authority portray that message while living their own lives. At the young age of 13, the result was that my heart was hardened like stone. I thought I hated God and Jesus. I started declaring to myself, "If that's what Jesus looks like, I'd rather go to hell with my friends." I continued on my path to destruction for several years, because of the lie that I believed, that Jesus hated me and I could never be "good enough," so why even try?

When I was 19, I became pregnant. I denied I was pregnant, willing it to go away. I decided I would have an abortion, because, after all, I was taught in public school it was "my body, my choice." I was at such a dark place that I heard everything through the lens of condemnation. While I cannot say for certain that a kind word would have changed my mind, I can say for certain that when I went to get my abortion, had there been people outside yelling the Gospel at me, telling me how wrong I was, telling me I was committing murder, telling me I'd better repent, then I would have grown even more hardened. That's what shoving the Gospel at someone does.

At age 26, when I was invited to a local church and I walked in those doors, I felt the kindness of Jesus and the love of Jesus through the people. It was the love that made all the difference, opening me to the Gospel and repentance.

Bob, another friend from the sidewalk, said:

> After only a few weeks of working with Shiela and Carrie, I quickly realized indignation or anger are exactly the wrong emotions to win people's hearts and minds. It's been said, "You catch more flies with honey than vinegar." Shiela's heartfelt actions and love-centered approach out on the sidewalk influenced my own sidewalk approach, as well as my own spiritual growth. It's not easy to approach strange people at a time of their great emotional stress, but Shiela made it look easy. This is because Shiela's personality is that of a person who has "never met a stranger," and her innate openness and friendliness serve as the model to emulate—not just out on the sidewalk, but also on our own journey of life. In summary, and perhaps this is baring my soul a little too much, I now see the abortion-minded woman as a damsel in distress rather than a woman who wants to commit a murder.

In my time on the sidewalk, I've witnessed thousands of people's emotions vary from one extreme to the other. Most people driving by honk in support, and a few honk in anger (those are generally easy to discern, as they display a corresponding middle finger). The people who stop to talk to us are usually there to encourage us in our ministry; often people pull up to ask what we're doing (i.e., which side we're on), and others stop because they're looking for an argument. Others yet have no idea it is an abortion clinic. People walking by can be indifferent, or praising us in support, occasionally on drugs and indecipherable or even downright verbally combative. Our accusers say we judge women, that we aren't looking out for their best interests, that we don't believe they should get to make their own choices. I say, we love women and want to educate, equip, and empower them to make the best choice for themselves, which never incudes abortion.

> *Don't repay evil for evil. Don't retaliate with insults when*
> *people insult you. Instead, pay them back with a blessing.*

77

That is what God has called you to do, and he will grant you his blessing.

1 Peter 3:9 (NLT)

Even though we encounter much negativity, God often sends wonderful people to cheer and uplift us, affirming the necessity and value of our ministry. I've seen people who appreciate our efforts bring donuts, sports drinks, waters, coffee, fast food gift cards, and cash donations. Many, many more simply stop to thank us and bless us for our efforts for the unborn. It lifts our spirits and brightens our day when God sends us these sweet messengers. One day, a very nice white man pulled up in his truck and told us, "I sure appreciate what y'all are doing out here. Unborn lives are very important. I adopted a child who was just three weeks old. She's four now, and sitting here in the backseat; she just had eye surgery." He was even a little emotional and teary-eyed, as he pointed her out to us. She waved at us, but couldn't see us because she still had bandages on from her surgery.

Many people are used to pro-lifers holding signs that say, "Honk for Life," so people recognize that we are out there and they honk loudly when driving by. It used to startle me quite a lot, but I got used to it and even enjoy it now, especially when the big trucks blare loudly.

Occasionally, though, like I mentioned, there are those who honk or scream, usually while giving us the middle-finger wave that we jokingly call the "California howdy," as we bless them in Jesus' name in return. And it's common for people to stop by and ask what exactly we're doing. They want to know our motivation: are we for the abortion clinic, or are we pro-lifers? If we're pro-lifers, are we condemning, or are we being helpful? Generally those conversations end well, as I explain our motivations and methods.

Then there are the people who come out to the sidewalk to spend some time and see what it's like to be out there—testing the waters, so to speak. They also run the emotional gamut. Often they feel a genuine desire to come, but some are just doing it for curiosity's sake. A few feel strongly called from God, but it's not their main ministry, or they just aren't able to fit it into their busy schedule. I understand that and certainly don't begrudge them — people have different seasons of life, like having a stressful job, caring for their children, or even caring for elderly parents. It would have been nearly impossible for me to do this ministry so often with little kids, or if I were still working more hours.

At times the people who come to volunteer have lost children to abortions; not all have gone through a post-abortive healing class, and it shows. Even if they have not experienced abortion first-hand, they may feel a palpable hatred towards the women and abortion workers going in. They outwardly display a pent-up rage, yelling at people driving in/out or at the abortion doctors. Honestly, that yelling makes me cringe inside, because even though I couldn't go through with an abortion myself and I don't feel I could work there, the hatred on display saddens my soul. I do my utmost to convey my heart to all the new volunteers that we need to show love to everyone. How else will they see the love of Jesus? God loves every one of them as much as He loves you and me. It's not my place to judge them on their actions, but to turn them towards Him so He can convict them in what is righteous and truthful.

God has softened my heart towards these abortion-minded women who feel they have no choice. And I have no idea what brought the workers to this place. Maybe they were desperate for a job, or maybe it was considered the norm in their family, or they honestly believe they're helping women. I do believe that somehow their eyes have been blinded to His truth that it is wrong to kill a child conceived in His image; I always pray that their eyes will be opened to discern His Truth. As is often said, "But by the grace of God, there go I."

Interacting with the Pro-abortion Counter-Protestors

If someone mistreats you because you are a Christian, don't curse him; pray that God will bless him.

Romans 12:14

If God is for us, who can be against us?

Romans 8:31b (NIV)

My first encounter with counter-protestors was the worst because it was so unexpected and I was caught totally off-guard. The very next morning, it was raining; I drove back to the clinic but parked a distance away to watch what was happening. Soon there was anxiety in the pit of my stomach. Paul, Janet and Bob were there with two very loud female counter-protestors. I observed those women harassing my friends, holding an electronic bullhorn near Bob's ear and following him around, while also holding a vulgar sign pointing to him. Paul texted to me, "Shiela, please call the police for us," which I did immediately. Very soon, a police officer came to intervene. Paul's shift was done, and he walked to my car as I was about to walk over to join Janet and Bob. He said, "Shiela, you don't have to go out there today. Yesterday was stressful enough for you—they can handle it if you need a break."

But, resolute, I decided that I was not going to let some rowdy, obnoxious protestors keep me from my ministry. "I'll be all right, Paul, but thank you—I appreciate your concern." No one would have blamed me, but I decided that God was going to be my Rock, and I would put my faith and trust in Him. They weren't going to keep me from doing the work He has called me to do. I trudged over to stand by Janet, and we calmly sang hymns; I quietly sang the lyrics to "I Love You, Lord," over and over. I quickly learned it was best to just ignore the pro-aborts completely, and pray blessings on them, that they learn their identity as children of the Most High God, instead of celebrating the atrocity of abortion. I felt a peace come over me, knowing that as distraught as I had been the day before, I was now doing what God intended, where I was meant to be.

They continued to hold their signs and rainbow flags, following Bob around for hours playing bagpipe music full blast on the bullhorn.

Janet writing:

When I walked up that first morning, I was caught by surprise because I didn't get Shiela's text to warn me. I immediately started praying and telling the Lord that He had to give me His peace. I told Him, "If You don't give me Your peace, I'm going to put her up out of my face." And once He gave me His peace, I was fine, and I was putting on the full armor of God. There was nothing she was going to say or do to upset me. Even blowing the cigarette smoke in my face and looking me in the eyes, asking me how I slept at night, trying to keep these women from doing what they wanted to do. I told her, nose to nose, "Take a deep look in my eyes; I sleep quite fine, thank you. I want you to know, greater is He who is in me than he who's in you, and I'm not afraid of who's in you." When I told her to look and asked, "What do you see?" she backed up. I said, "I will not be moved, no matter what," that first day, and I held my ground.

Then the Lord brought to my mind the song about singing a hallelujah in the presence of my enemies, so I started singing it.

81

After that episode, she'd get close, but she never got nose to nose with me again. And any time they've come since, I immediately put on my spiritual armor and say, "God, give me Your peace," and then I'm good.

I would love to say that is the only encounter I've had with pro-abortion protestors, but sadly, they came back the next day and many times since. They mostly come out for special occasions or Saturdays. Each time, they're like an irritating fly that doesn't easily go away.

The pro-aborts especially seem to enjoy coming to taunt Catholics while they stand or sit silently praying their rosaries. They mock, they scorn, they twist Scripture, they lie—they sound like what you would imagine Satan to be like, non-stop with no new material, just switching it up a little, being very loud and obnoxious all along the way. They yell things like, "You should be ashamed of yourselves! God doesn't want you out here judging women!"

The protestors have continued to come intermittently ever since, especially on Saturdays, when I am typically not there. They have shown up occasionally during the week, though, to create havoc. Once, they pulled up in the driveway near us and blared out the Lord's Prayer with the megaphone, replacing most of the words with expletives. I just sat in my chair and ignored them, so they soon got bored and left. But they have jumped in front of me when I tried to talk to women who stopped to talk to me, and screamed at the women, "Keep driving—don't stop!"

Sadly, they include their little children as well, indoctrinating them into their evil doings, engaging them with drawing chalk obscenities on the driveway, as the adults dress up in tiger and unicorn costumes, displaying rainbow flags and signs that say, "Abortion workers are heroes," "Abortion saves lives," "Honk for choice," and "Forced birth is white supremacy."

What I Say on the Sidewalk

Never tire of doing what is good.

2 Thessalonians 3:13 (NIV)

Always work enthusiastically for the Lord, for you know that nothing you do for the Lord is ever useless.

1 Corinthians 15:58b (NLT)

The main question I'm asked by the people I mentor is "What do you say to the women coming in for abortions?" And the truth is, I say whatever God says through me. Usually, I feel I'm completely inadequate, and I just pray that God managed to use something that they saw or heard to change their minds. I often ask, "Are you at the right location? Are you looking for the abortion clinic? May I ask what brings you here?" They usually respond appropriately, although some don't want to answer at all, and some even argue with me that it's not an abortion clinic. When that happens, I politely reply, "Yes it is, and they perform an average of over 40 each week. They've done more than 100,000 abortions here."

Women come for hormonal birth control and other gyne-cological services like pap smears for cervical cancer screening and STD (sexually transmitted disease) tests. Some come after a miscar-riage, for a D&C, and some are not abortion-minded but just want an ultrasound. I try to always let them know that a PRC (pregnancy resource center) right across the street also has free pregnancy tests, where no one will be having abortions while they get their test done. The PRC also has many other OB/GYN (obstetric and gyneco-logical) services, all of which are free. Quite often, one or more people each day will leave at that point; they either don't want to enter an abortion facility or they want to take advantage of the PRC's free services. Sometimes they meant to go to the PRC in the first place, and we happily point them in that direction.

Several times, older patients have stopped to say with much fondness that they've been with their doctor inside for decades for gynecological reasons; one even said that Dr. One had saved her life many years ago when she tried to abort her own baby. She just couldn't understand why we'd be out there on the sidewalk when he was doing such great work.

Once a white woman stopped after she had dropped off her friend, saying, "I don't believe in abortion, but my friend lives several hours away, and she had a botched abortion. She asked me to help her, and I would have never taken her to have the abortion, but I brought her here to save her life."

The longer conversations ensue when they affirm they are there for an abortion. Women's reasoning for having abortions are often as follows: I can't afford this. The timing isn't right. The father isn't around. I have other kids. I just made a mistake one night. I'm in school. My parents will be upset. I just had a baby. I have a special needs child already. I'm in an abusive relationship. I'm scared because of medical complications.

I have many talking points, but since time is precious, I quickly try to give them our informational brochures that focus on the mother and her well-being. The main brochure has many resources on local PRCs, abortion pill reversal, adoption, etc. I generally also include the two brochures I created and explain them as well; one is for post-abortive counseling, and the other contains 12 true, compelling stories I heard from friends—eight had abortions and four did not. I never know when another car is going to come, and I cannot block the driveway, so I have to be ready to quickly get out of the way.

I often give a woman what I call a "mom blessing bag" and congratulate her on being a mother. The see-through plastic baggie contains a pair of baby socks, booties, a hat, or other such new little baby item, a Gospel tract, candy, a printed Scripture of Psalms 139:15-17, and other pregnancy resources. I have Spanish versions as well. Occasionally they will reject the gift, but usually they accept it. Many people have donated these and other items for me to hand out, which is a huge blessing. If a mother has lost a child to abortion or is coming in for another reason, I have other appropriate gifts, and they smile appreciatively. When we can form a friendly bond, it helps them stop and talk to me in the future, even if they do go through with the abortion.

Quite often, the men are the ones who are visibly as upset or more upset than the women. Many say they feel they don't have a choice in the matter, even though they are the father. I have a special brochure I give them, called "For Men Only," and I empower them to help their partners make a decision for life. I tell them, "That is your child also. It looks like you, and it might have your eyes or your nice smile. Doing this will negatively affect your relationship. This is not the best thing for the woman's health and well-being. She won't be the same person afterwards. If you truly want what's best for her, try to talk her out of it."

When I am blessed to have more time to chat with the car's occupants, I may compliment them on their beautiful smiles, hair, eyes, or anything else that stands out to me. Typically, they thank me, and then I tell them that their baby will have their same beautiful features. I might tell them my mother's story, especially if they already have had children. I say, "If you go through with this abortion, you will not come out the same person—it will change who you are and negatively impact your life forever."

I do try to engage them in conversation, and I will sometimes ask them questions about why they want to have the abortion. They often stay very quiet, and since I know my time is limited, I keep talking as long as they will listen or until another car comes and I have to step back. I just pray that God will use something I say to trigger a positive response: "Don't sell yourself short—you can do this, you're stronger than you think, and there are people here who are willing to help you through this."

Eventually I ask, "Do you believe in God?" If they answer that they do, then my follow-up question is, "Do you believe that He is bigger than your problems and that He can handle anything?" They usually do, so I ask them to really think and pray about what He wants for their lives. "He does not want you to do this. He created this new miracle that's inside of you. It's not the best thing for your body and your life. Your chances of cancer can increase, and it is destructive to your mental and emotional health as well."

Some people tell us they will think about it, and they leave the clinic; we call this a "hopeful." Other times, they decide to turn around and not even enter, or they drive out and tell us they've definitely changed their minds; we call this a "save." Sometimes, instead a friend, cousin, spouse, mother, etc. will happily stop and tell us. I've seen saves more than 30 times on the days I've been there, but I'm sure the actual number is much higher; many people leave after less than an hour but don't stop to tell us why. Regardless, we rejoice and praise God each time!

The Stories

On my third week of ministry, a black girl was driving in with her two friends and asked me, "Is this the abortion clinic? Because I don't want to have this baby. I've got to hurry to get to my appointment." She took my information and I quickly shared the story of my birth, although she seemed like she didn't want to hear it. In fact, when I stated that I was born dead, she retorted twice, "But you're here now!" She quickly drove off, but within a few seconds I saw the car come back. She stopped the car and exclaimed, "I'm not having the abortion!" Her entire demeanor had changed! She and her friends were so happy when they left. I was crying tears of joy and decided this ministry was amazing.

This was the first of many saves, but it's still one of the most impactful I've experienced. To see the faces on those girls go from such glum and despair to incredible hopefulness and happiness is a miracle to behold. And to think, all it took was someone to speak truth and light to them. These women are usually in a very rough patch in their lives, and they've come to the clinic out of desperation, because they feel they are completely out of options. A volunteer simply being available to talk and pray in nonjudgmental love can make a huge difference in their lives.

A white couple stopped on their way driving in so the male driver could take candy from me. He said, "Yes, we're here for an abortion," when I asked if they were at the right place. I handed him our local tri-fold, the brochure for men only, and the abortion stories. I briefly explained them, and I also gave them a mom blessing bag. They said she was eight weeks along. I said, "Even if you go through with this abortion, you'll still carry the memory of the baby." She was crying, looking away a lot, and she didn't speak. They zoomed off into the parking lot, but they came back out just five minutes later. They stopped to talk (he was on the phone) and told us they were going to keep the baby. I tried to give her a congratulations card with my info in it along with a baby quilt and said, "We would love to keep in contact with you and give you a baby shower gift."

She gestured that she didn't want anything, so I left her alone while he said, "She's overwhelmed right now." She was crying and unable to speak, but she definitely had decided to choose life!

A black couple stopped to talk on their way in; she told me, "I'm coming for an abortion because a baby will affect my career in law enforcement; we already have a three-month-old girl." She pointed to the backseat, saying, "I had to quit my last job when I was pregnant with her." I told them my story, gave them information, and showed them the baby model. I asked, "Do you believe in God?" When they responded positively, I explained, "His timing is perfect, and He can handle anything—you should trust Him to handle this for you; you shouldn't take matters into your own hands, and you shouldn't do this to your child's sibling." They went in but came out nearly an hour and a half later to tell me they changed their minds and would keep the baby. Jack was preaching with a speaker over the fence that day, and I asked if they heard him while they were in the parking lot. They said they had. Whatever it was that worked to change their minds that day, all of us out there rejoiced.

A black mother and her pregnant 17-year-old daughter drove in and stopped to see what I had to say. I gave them all my brochures and then some! They were open and listened as I told my story, and I said she wouldn't know how much she'd love the baby until she saw it. I showed the fetal model and gave her a mom blessing bag and a little handmade ribbon cross. I asked if they believed in God, and when they responded positively, I asked if they believed He was in control and if He could handle their problems. The mother looked at the daughter, who said, "I think I'll keep it after all." We were all joyful then! We exchanged contact information, and I gave her a handmade baby blanket. Although I had told them about the PRC, they drove away without stopping there. I followed up with a text to the mother that evening:

> Hello! This is Shiela Miller, the redhead from outside the clinic today. Are you both doing okay? I was so thrilled to get to talk to you both.

She answered:

> We are, and I'm glad we talked to you today. They asked me not to stop, but I'm so glad God said different. Thank you for helping us decide what we already knew.

Her pregnant daughter's story:

> My mother and I came to the abortion clinic because I was only 17 and the baby's father didn't want to be a part of the picture—he actually wanted me to have an abortion. We saw you at the driveway and stopped because we wanted to see what you had to say. While you were talking, I realized that the baby didn't ask to be here, and I shouldn't take his life because I made a mistake. I'm happy and I think it was a good decision to keep the baby. I would like to tell other pregnant mothers that they shouldn't have an abortion because once you see the baby on the ultrasound for the first time and see its heartbeat, it's just the best feeling!

I asked this young woman, "Why did you choose life?"
She answered, "Thou shalt not kill."

After she had her baby boy, I asked her how she felt about her decision. She's in love with him and very glad she decided to keep him; the baby's father is even coming and helping her out now.

A white woman stopped for a brochure, but she had to drive off quickly because someone was pulling up behind her. She stopped to talk to us when she came out. "I decided to go in and pay for an ultrasound, but I'm keeping this baby, although the baby's father doesn't know. It was a one-night stand, and I'll be doing this on my own." We told her we'd love to keep in contact for baby shower gifts, and we exchanged information. What she said next was amazing. "I came here last year to have the surgical abortion, and someone out here gave me a pair of baby booties on my way in. I kept looking at them and thought to myself, 'What are you doing?' Then I knew I couldn't go through with it. My little boy is five months old now." How exciting that she had changed her mind at the last minute. Someone from our ministry had given her baby booties on the way in, and she couldn't go through with it! It's wonderful to find out about saves after the fact!

Connecting with her three months later, I found out more of her backstory:

A dangerous man I knew forced me at gunpoint to have sex with him, and I became pregnant. I already had two children and I was scared; I just didn't know how having this child would affect me, so I decided to have an abortion. When I came to the clinic, a woman gave me a see-through bag with blue baby booties. I went inside the clinic, paid, and did the urine test. But when I went into the clinic, I had accidentally grabbed that bag instead of my phone. I sat and stared at those booties and thought to myself, "What are you doing?" I realized I couldn't go through with it and ran out of the clinic, nearly having an anxiety attack. Now I have a happy

89

eight-month-old boy that I just love; he's my buddy, and we do everything together. I'm so thankful I chose to keep him, and I don't believe in abortion as an answer.

A black woman stopped to speak with me while Carrie and Bob were praying on the sidewalk. I didn't realize that she was coming for an abortion, and I called Carrie over. "Carrie, come here to share your natural family planning information." Carrie came over and engaged her right away, commenting, "I like your sticker on your car." It said, ALL THINGS ARE POSSIBLE WITH GOD. Well, all things were possible that day, as we convinced her to go across the street to the PRC. Carrie went with her and kept in touch. We were thrilled to find out she had been pregnant and chose life for her son. Months later, I was blessed to assist the day when Carrie and others hosted a baby shower for her, and I also visited with her when he was a week old. She told me her story:

> I was coming in for an abortion because I wasn't planning on having any more kids—I already had two and I thought I was done. I stopped when I saw Shiela out on the sidewalk because I was very interested in what she was going to say. I ended up changing my mind and decided to keep the baby because the Bible says, "Thou shalt not kill." I don't believe in abortion; I never have. If she hadn't been there that day, I still think I wouldn't have been able to go through with it. I would like to tell abortion-minded women, think twice before you do it—don't just do it. And if you feel like you can't take care of it, let it be adopted instead of just killing it; it's a human being. The baby has to be here; your predicament is not its problem.

I was able to intercept a black lady, who was very unsure of what to do; she was pregnant, already had two girls, and had just had an abortion in the spring. She said she needed to make a decision quickly because soon it would be too late, and they were strapped financially. I gave her lots of literature, told her that the PRC had abortion recovery classes, told her my story, and gave her a mom blessing bag. She said, "I think I was meant to meet you here. I'm not going to go in there after all." We exchanged phone numbers to keep in touch, and I was able to bring her gifts and see her sweet baby, which ended up being a third girl, whom she loved very much.

A Hispanic woman drove up and we chatted in Spanish. I gave her the typical information, and she drove away soon after. But she came back in, and I asked, "Why are you back here?" She said she was there for an abortion and showed me $700 cash that she had in her hands. Her credit card hadn't worked, so she had gone to borrow money from friends for an "emergency." She said that she was feeling too sick to work and she already had a son. I told her, "No, you should not do this!" She decided to go in to park, and then she walked back out to me. On the way, she had to stop to vomit because of bad morning sickness. We called to connect her to a Spanish-speaking worker from a local pregnancy resource center, and even though she had to stop again to vomit more, she stayed on the phone quite a while. The PRC worker convinced her to come see them right away and then their group spent the afternoon helping her. She chose life for her second son that day.

[*Translated from Spanish*] When I first suspected I was pregnant, I went to a PRC to take a pregnancy test. When the lady told me I was pregnant, she asked me if I was planning to keep it or give it up for adoption. Although I told her I was planning on having the baby, I secretly planned to have an abortion. My situation was not good when I became pregnant with David. I was not with his father, and the

91

pregnancy was unplanned. I physically felt bad and was not able to work, so the financial struggles were real; I already had an eight-year-old son to care for, and I was only 22 years old. I felt in my heart a voice that kept repeating, "I'm going to do this, I'm going to do this," regarding having an abortion.

Next, I looked up the abortion clinic and went to sign the papers and start the procedures. They wouldn't take my credit card, so I left to get cash. The redhead [Shiela] asked me to talk, and I wanted to hear what she had to say. She encouraged me to realize that I should have the baby and told me not to go through with the abortion. I came out and talked to her more, and I started to cry. I went right away to a PRC in town that had a Spanish translator available that day, and the ladies there took very good care of me; they made me feel very special.

I am so very happy to have chosen life. I would like to tell other women to have their children, because although I don't want any more children, if I were to become pregnant again, I would not commit that error to think of having an abortion. Children are wonderful, and I've lived a beautiful experience with them.

I invited this mother, who was due in four months, to a bilingual church. She enjoyed the service immensely. Afterwards, while connecting with some members there, one of the female pastors asked her if she would like to accept Christ as her Savior, and she said she would. Through tears, I witnessed her declaring the Sinner's Prayer, and I realized I had not only helped save her baby's life but her eternal life as well. Since then, I have kept in contact with her on a regular basis and have many photos with her and her sweet child.

Little David came into the world in March 2020, and I was bummed not to be able to go visit him and his mother in the hospital because of pandemic restrictions. But the birth went well and they were healthy—I was able to visit and take gifts when they got home two days later. Valerie visited the following day with a large cash donation gathered from her Catholic prayer group, and they continued to help her until she was financially stable. I have enjoyed a lasting friendship with this mother, and often give thanks to God that I have the ability to speak Spanish!

This mother and son have since visited us on the sidewalk a couple of times on her days off. Once she was able to speak in Spanish to a Hispanic woman there on the driveway, and she believes the woman may have changed her mind about having the abortion. She also recently talked a friend out of having an abortion and then blessed her by giving her friend a baby shower. She has an amazing testimony of keeping her child and now is convincing others to keep theirs as well!

Even during the pandemic we were able to assist women who truly wanted help. As a black lady drove into the driveway, I stood up in the mulch to wave and speak to her. She stopped and I stayed far away while asking her the usual questions: Was she in the right place? Was she looking for the abortion clinic? She hesitantly said that she was, so I asked, "Can I text you some information? They can help you across the street with a free pregnancy test and ultrasound. I'll walk over to introduce you." She did give me her phone number and agreed to go across the street with me. We went over and I chatted with her a little about her name, to try to relax her, because she looked like a deer in headlights. She was smiling when I left her with them, and I also texted her our informative brochures. She didn't respond at the time, but months later I discovered that she had decided to keep her sweet baby. I met her, gave her some gift cards, and saw her little boy.

Sometimes plans are foiled, and women end up not having an abortion because of physical or legal constraints. Sometimes they just have very persistent family members and/or friends.

An unhappy-looking black woman stopped to speak with me while she was driving into the clinic. She was able to speak with me for quite a while uninterrupted. She said, "My daughter is here to have an abortion, and I want to try to talk to her, because I don't want her to do this. Her boyfriend at first wanted her to have the abortion, but he's changed his mind and he wants her to have the baby, too. She actually took the abortion pill and did it correctly, but it didn't work."

I said, "Wow, that seems like a sign you should keep your baby when that happens."

"I know, right?" she answered. "I was molested and raped when I was only 13, and I feel it was necessary for me to have an abortion, but my daughter is in her 30s and she doesn't need to be doing this. She's in the position to take care of this child with my help and his support. She's a grown adult. And her sister just died a few months ago and really wanted her to have a child—her last one ended in miscarriage."

I armed her with information, and she entered the parking lot. A few minutes later, she returned, saying, "My daughter won't talk to me; I talked to the boyfriend, and he said she's going through with it."

"Listen," I said, "You need to go back in there and talk to her. Give it another shot! You have to live with the consequences of this day for the rest of your life. That's your grandchild, so don't you want to know that you did everything in your power to save it?" She was crying and finally she backed her car up into the parking lot again to give it another try. Sadly, she came out yet again, crying even harder.

She said, "She came out of the clinic to talk to me, and I told her that I would help her with the child. She's in school right now and the timing is bad, but she's had a miscarriage before. I told her she might never have another child after this."

Janet and I strongly encouraged her to get post-abortive help for herself from the PRC so that she could heal and better help her own daughter afterwards. She agreed and then completely left the facility.

I asked people to continue to pray, because there's always hope someone might change her mind. Well, several hours later I received a phone call from the mother. "My daughter changed her mind! She's keeping the baby!" Praise God for answered prayers! Empowering her to go back in to that clinic a second time helped her daughter realize that she would have support, so she changed her mind and kept the baby after all! This woman's mother was thrilled because it was her birthday that week, and she considered the grandbaby to be a wonderful gift. Praise to God for answered prayers! I met with that grandmother a month later to give her gift cards from our generous pro-life family, which she greatly appreciated. Here's what she had to say:

> My daughter went for an abortion because she was afraid that the baby's father would leave her. I think it changed her mind once I talked to her. If it hadn't been for me going there and talking to her, she would have had that abortion. I think by me going back, turning to go back, and her knowing how I felt, I think that's what gave her the change of heart. I truly think that she felt my feelings after I got to talk to her. Because if I hadn't gone back, we wouldn't be having a baby right now. She lost her sister two months earlier; that sister had wanted her to have a baby. This baby girl will have a similar name in memory of her aunt.

After the baby was born, the baby's mother said the following:

> I had an intuition that the baby's father would go back to being with his other kids' mother, and he did by the time I was seven months along. I worried when I got pregnant that after taking abortion pills, my baby would be sick or something would be wrong. And I felt like I may end up alone. I feared becoming a single mother and not being able to finish nursing school. Well, my baby is healthy, so thank God for that. Nothing is wrong with her, and she brings me so much joy. However, my intuition was right: I am basically doing it all on my own as far as waking up in the middle of

the night to feed, taking her to doctor appointments, early mornings. Not to mention I will still have to find a way to manage working both full-time and finishing school as a single mom. Overall, I am still worried about my future and sometimes depressed, but I can say since having my daughter I am so in love. She is my pride and joy. All I can do is pray everything will fall into place. And I know that my ambitious personality is even stronger. I cannot and will not let her down.

A young black woman stopped to speak with me on the way into the clinic; I told her everything I could and gave her a lot of information and gifts. She was very quiet but still listened. She said that the timing wasn't good now and she'd had an abortion a couple of years ago. I called Janet over, and she said, "Sweetie, you'll regret it right away if you do this. I had an abortion years ago and I would have killed myself if I hadn't been of the belief that I'd go straight to hell." When the woman told me she was around three months pregnant, I gave her a 12-week fetal model, and she kept holding it and looking at it. She seemed very nervous at the prospect of having a baby, and I assured her, "You can do this—you are strong!" After nearly an hour, she decided to go on in. Thankfully, I stayed around longer than normal that day, and when she drove back out an hour later, she stopped to joyfully show me her ultrasound photo.[5] She said, "I'm 15 weeks along, so I can't have the procedure done there after all." We were thankful and instantly gave her handmade baby gifts and congratulations. She was grinning from ear to ear.

I spoke to a young black couple on their way in, giving them the normal items, and they stopped again on the way out. They

---

[5] (Photo displayed on page 47)

were laughing uproariously. Very curious, I asked, "What is going on?"

The female in the passenger seat answered, "They made me mad because they wouldn't let me get the abortion, so I left."

Flabbergasted, I asked, "Why?"

She said, "They wouldn't let me do it because I signed the form online at 3 a.m. and it hadn't been 24 hours yet, so they said I'd have to come back tomorrow. We're not doing that—we don't want to see them again." We exchanged information so I could give her a baby present, because she was actually happy to keep the baby. She had just been nervous that her parents wouldn't think she was taking her career seriously, and she wasn't sure how the father really felt. We kept in touch, and months later I was able to take her baby gifts and see this precious child in the hospital when she was just a day old. I'll never forget seeing that little girl, and being incredibly joyful to be a little part of her story.

Those wonderful testimonies of babies saved from death are part of what keeps us going back out to the clinic day after day, month after month, year after year. We are again uplifted and regenerated for more of this spiritual battle, to help mothers' hearts one by one. But not all of the stories on the sidewalk have happy endings. The truth is that there are at least ten sad stories for every happy one. I've seen the aftermath of abortion up close and personal, and it's not pretty. So, so many times I've seen sad, young teen girls and women in their twenties and thirties curled up, looking sick, or crying. Anne Huff encouraged me to write a post-abortive healing brochure that we could hand out, which I did in 2019.[35]

It has amazed me how many people have stopped to talk to me after they went through with an abortion. I really believe that they realize that I'm not out there to judge them, and they stop again because they just want a moment of comfort while going through their sorrow.

One of the stories that really tore at my heartstrings was a distraught white mother who stopped to speak with me for quite a while on her way in. "I'm not in a good financial situation to have this baby, and I've already had one abortion. I know it's a sin, and I know I'm destined for hell as it is." She was so downtrodden and full of grief and despair that she thought her life couldn't get any worse by committing this act a second time.

I shared the Gospel and did everything I could think of to encourage her to keep her baby, saying, "I don't care what anyone has told you, you do *not* have to go to hell because of this! Yes, God is perfect and you have sinned, but He wants to have a relationship with you if you just choose Him! Jesus paid the price for your sin and died so you don't have to, if you repent and turn to Him as your Lord and Master. Make a good choice now and don't compound your grief. You can stop this cycle now. Choose life!"

She finally drove on in, and I supposed she went through with the abortion, but I prayed she didn't.

> *He longs for all to be saved and to understand this truth:*
> *That God is on one side and all the people on the other side,*
> *and Christ Jesus, Himself man, is between them to bring*
> *them together, by giving His life for all mankind. This is*
> *the message which at the proper time God gave to the*
> *world.*
>
> *1 Timothy 2:4-6*

Some stories are bittersweet or downright sad, and occasionally I am able to use some of my experiences to connect with the women. One young white woman stopped to talk to me as she was driving in. Even though she was there for an abortion, she took all of my information. I asked her, "Has anyone congratulated you yet on being a mother?" She said no, accepting a mom blessing bag from me. She then said, "I don't believe in abortion, but I have a life-threatening medical condition." Right then, a car came up behind and I had to back off quickly. I said to Anne, "I'm so sad I didn't

98

have a chance to give her the information we have on the high-risk doctor."

Thankfully, she came out about 15 minutes later and told me, "I decided to keep my baby after all." I then asked her to pull over into an adjacent parking lot so I could speak more with her. She said, "I'm just so scared because of my health condition." I proceeded to exchange phone numbers with her and gave her the high-risk doctor's contact information.

I said, "We like to keep in contact and give baby shower gifts when women choose life." Then I told her my personal story and why I was out there, which seemed to touch her. After visiting the PRC across the street, she drove out and gave a great big smile and thumbs up! I was so happy for her. Then she returned my text some days later:

> Shiela, I'm sorry I haven't answered you sooner. I really appreciate all the help you and the PRC gave me—I'm just so grateful! It breaks my heart to tell you, but I miscarried the baby just days after I met you. I'm sad about it, but I believe God is in charge. Also, I want to thank you for helping me make the right choice—I was about to commit a terrible sin against an innocent child. Thank you so much for helping me and for all you do!!! You saved me from sinning and I love you for that.

I answered her:

> I'm so sorry, and I'm crying for you, but yes I'm thankful that you didn't take the life of your baby. I miscarried one time as well. Please realize it's a true baby, and it was a loss, so give it a name; God has it safe in heaven, love you so much!

She responded:

> Thank you for everything. I'm sorry for your loss! I love you so much!!

Speaking mostly in Spanish, one day a Hispanic lady told me, "I desperately want to keep my baby, but my obstetrician said to abort it because I'm six weeks and it doesn't seem to have a heartbeat. I actually came here for second opinion; Dr. One told me that sometimes it's difficult to see that early, so I should wait two weeks and then come back to check again. He's going to do that next ultrasound for free."

Noticing her rosary hanging from her rearview mirror, I asked her, "Are you Catholic?" After she replied affirmatively, I asked her, "Can my Catholic friends and I pray for you?" She readily agreed, and we exchanged contact information. A few days later when I texted her, sadly, she said she had lost her baby the day before. She also texted:

> Thank you very much for caring about me. That day I found you I felt so calm and happy to know that someone who does not know me was praying for me and my baby, I wish God bless you always.

A black woman stopped for me as she was driving in; I offered her a gift bag, and she took it. Then I asked, "Are you in the right place—you're looking for the abortion clinic?" She nodded, and I asked, "Have you been here before?" When she again nodded her affirmation, I realized she was coming for her three-week ultra-sound check-up after taking the abortion pill. She confirmed my hunch, saying, "I already have two children and I had to make a difficult decision." At that point, I asked how she was getting along and if I could give her some information on post-abortive healing, since many women have a difficult time afterwards. She accepted it and replied, "I'm sad."

I said, "My friend Janet would have committed suicide after losing a child to abortion, but refrained only because of her faith at the time, thinking she'd go straight to hell. And Anne's niece had tried to feel better by having another child, and then going down a path of drugs, which only led to her committing suicide when the negative feelings were just too overwhelming. You can go right across the street to that PRC [pointing] to take post-abortive healing classes. I care about you and your recovery. Will you please call them?" She replied that she would, and I have prayed that she and the many others in identical circumstances that I have spoken with would also go to receive the much-needed healing.

One day, a white woman stopped to speak with me before she drove into the clinic. I asked, "Hi, are you looking for the abortion clinic?"

She answered, "Yes, I already have a special needs child and he takes up 100% of my time. I don't have the finances either. I already have to work extra to pay for his therapy. My OB said my chances were very high of my next child also being autistic, and I just can't handle that extra burden in my life right now." She did proceed to take information from me, but nothing I said seemed to penetrate her mindset.

A while later, her mother drove by and also stopped to talk. She was crying, "My daughter's not married, and she's in an abusive relationship with a man who isn't the father of the child she already has. I work full-time, so I can't help her out with another baby. Neither one of us want her to have the abortion, but having this baby just isn't something that she's able to do—she has to get an abortion. We just can't find another way out!"

I answered, "I don't have all the answers, but God can handle anything going on in your lives. Have you considered adoption? There are so many people willing and able to provide a loving home for the baby and it would be a blessing to them. You should at least talk to someone over at the PRC to see what help they can offer, instead of going through with this awful choice that you'll both live to regret for the rest of your lives."

Sadly, she did go through with her abortion. I saw them a couple of weeks later when they drove in for the checkup; they didn't stop to talk but rolled down their window for a greeting on the way in.

Janet and I (with Bob present and praying) spoke to a young black couple going into the clinic for an abortion because the "timing wasn't right." Like so many others, they were in college at the time. They were attentive and respectful, taking all our information and a mom blessing bag, and listening to what we had to say. I told them both, "Even though she isn't far along, she's still a mother." We prayed they would change their minds and come out, but she took the abortion pill. They stopped on the way out to speak to us. The young man said, "I'm so sorry, but we did not listen to your advice, so we'd like to give you back your information." I said, "Well, please at least keep the post-abortive healing brochure." We were incredibly sad when they left.

I was shocked when, three weeks later, the same young man walked out to the sidewalk to speak with me. He said, "We're back for her post-abortive ultrasound check-up, just to make sure the pill worked properly and there was nothing left inside growing or getting infected in her uterus." We had a half-hour-long conversation, and much to my surprise, he said, "We do regret having the abortion now; she's having a very difficult time. Everything you told us was completely spot-on. I'm a medical student, and I had done the research. She was only about three weeks along, so I didn't think it would be a big deal. When you gave her the baby gift and said that she was a mother already, you were right. I didn't think so at the time, but that motherly instinct took over and she was having nightmares, repeating to herself, 'I killed it, I killed it.'"

He also talked about the dread of coming to the abortion clinic. He described how he felt a darkness there, saying also, "The staff was not friendly. They walk around with their heads down like they're doing something wrong. They also tell people on the phone not to talk to any of you on the way in. I really appreciate and approve of what you all do out here. I want to use this knowledge in the future to let others know that it's really a baby and it will impact the mother to abort it."

I shared with him the truth I knew, that his baby lives, and that one day—thanks to the redeeming grace of God—they all would be reunited in heaven. We kept in contact, and thankfully, they continued to say they were both doing well. I pray for them whenever I remember their story.

Over the past three years, I have often been amazed at how open and sharing many patients have with me, a complete stranger. Besides their personal stories, they have also told me what they have observed while inside the abortion clinic—the employees, the protocols, the services provided, and their costs.

My friends and I rejoice every time a woman chooses life, and often we keep in touch with the mother and give her baby gifts. Some have come to pro-life events that included blessing them with a large baby shower. The photos that follow are of me with some of the women and their newborn babies from the previous stories.

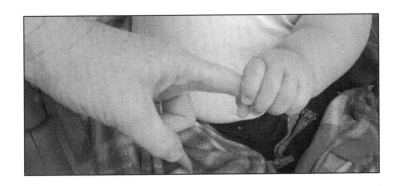

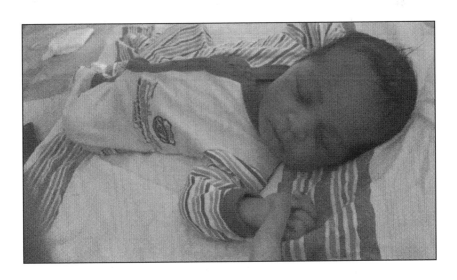

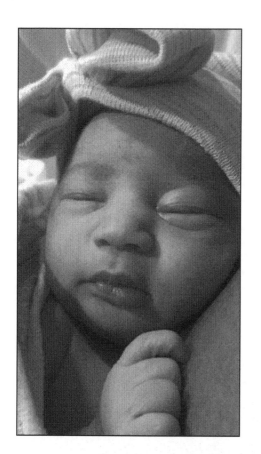

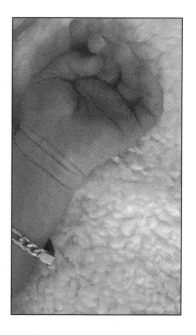

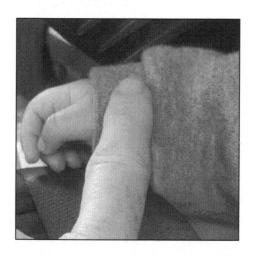

Part Four

Forming a Connection
at the Fence

8

Connecting with Gifts

For if you give, you will get! Your gift will return to you in full and over-flowing measure.

Luke 6:38

Don't just pretend to love others. Really love them. Hate what is wrong. Hold tightly to what is good. Love each other with genuine affection and take delight in honoring each other.

Romans 12:9-10 (NLT)

Three things will last forever—faith, hope, and love—and the greatest of these is love.

1 Corinthians 13:13 (NLT)

Shiela writing:

There are different camps of thought by pro-lifers about giving gifts to abortion workers. Some say something like, "Try to reach out to them in any way you can to show God's love." Although the language might vary somewhat, the others say, "Hell, no! Absolutely do not reward them for killing babies!" I've heard both arguments; seeing firsthand the positive reception of our gift-giving at Christmastime, I chose the former camp. Maybe it comes more naturally to me, because I am a giver, which I learned a few years ago after taking a spiritual questionnaire. On my own, I gradually decided to continue in the overall tradition of giving during the rest of the year as well. If my prayer every morning is to be a blessing to others, why wouldn't I want to brighten an abortion worker's day also? My sidewalk friends marveled as they observed how a couple of the workers were responding to me, especially an African American woman named Dionne, who became increasingly friendly over time. I intentionally thought about ways I could give. What candy does she like? What gifts would be appropriate? What messages should I text?

First though, let me explain that my friend Carrie had been a very sweet example by giving gifts to the workers at Christmas since 2015. She simply called the abortion clinic and asked if she could bring the gifts inside. As luck would have it, Dionne answered the phone that first year and gave her permission. In the years after that, some of Carrie's pro-life friends would help assemble the presents. Often, they were beautiful baskets of goodies with colorful store-bought and homemade items and cards. It was always a joyous time, knowing we were sending Christmas joy and love into a dark place.

For Christmas 2015, I prepared some gift bags in faith for the employees, not knowing if I'd get permission to bring them in. When I returned to my car after my time on the sidewalk the next morning, I called the abortion facility number, and Dionne answered. She was very nice and said I could bring the gifts in, so I drove my car into their parking lot and brought the gifts inside the clinic. Since then I have been able to talk to or share friendly hand waves with Dionne, some of her family, and some other employees on several occasions when they enter or exit. I believe that even though we disagree, it can only help for us to be kind to each other. Each employee is unique, with unique beliefs and unique reasons why they work there. Our job is really to love, care, and pray rather than to judge or change anyone. I was able to introduce Shiela and Dionne, and Shiela, being more personable than I am, has developed a good relationship with Dionne. I am very thankful for our "sidewalk family": those of us who pray and counsel, those moms and families we have helped and offered help to (some of whom we are keeping in touch with), and those employees we care about.

Shiela has really helped and taught all of us more about carrying God's hope and joy in our hearts and exuding it to others as we trust Him to speak to them.

—Carrie

Dionne writing:

When Carrie called the clinic that day and asked if she could bring in something that she had bought for us, luckily enough I was the one that answered the phone. I said, "Sure, why not?" I mean, I figured there couldn't be any harm in that. And it was really very nice of her that year, and in years since with the other ladies, to put those baskets together for us, especially when some of my coworkers can be rude and unappreciative. But I appreciate everything that they do and give us because I know it's coming from the heart, and the baskets are really nice. I appreciate it every year, and believe it or not, Dr. Two appreciates it, too.

A while back, my son came to me and said, "Mama, I gave your number to the lady out there," and the first thing that came to my mind was, "Why? Why give her my number? Why didn't you give her yours? You were the one out there talking to them." He replied, "She seemed real nice, and I just figured that maybe she could talk to you, and you all could go from there." I said, "Well, okay, if she reaches out I'll respond. I won't hesitate or be rude." And I did. I responded to Carrie and we ended up texting back and forth a little. At first, I was ticked at my son for giving my number out, but it was all good.

Carrie and Ingrid bringing Christmas presents

Christmas basket of goodies

9

Texting Connection

The LORD directs our steps, so why try to understand everything along the way?

Proverbs 20:24 (NLT)

"My thoughts are nothing like your thoughts," says the LORD. "And my ways are far beyond anything you could imagine.

Isaiah 55:8 (NLT)

The week prior to Christmas 2018

Shiela's thoughts: Dionne's son Desmond stopped to chat with me for the first time. He said, "I don't like abortions, and I won't send anyone in there. I stopped to talk to you because we have a lot we can agree on. I have a baby girl myself and I love her so much." He proudly showed me photos of her on his phone. He was very friendly and seemed very receptive as he took pro-life information from me. I was thrilled to get to talk to a relative of an abortion worker. I didn't know Dionne personally, but Carrie had told me who she was. Her son was sweet, and I was honestly just pleased to make a connection with someone going into the clinic on a regular basis. Maybe he would tell his mom that we had talked and that we were nice people. Maybe she would stop to talk one day. Any small step was a triumph in my book.

Dionne's thoughts: My son didn't even tell me he stopped to talk to Shiela—I had no idea.

Valentine's Day 2019

Shiela's thoughts: Like I mentioned, I had decided to give whatever gifts were appropriate to abortion workers and/or patients, and always looked for an opportunity. Valentine's Day was a great excuse, and I readily discovered that Dionne liked chocolate. That day was the first time she had ever stopped for me. I was waving to her, holding out some chocolate, as I said loudly, "I have some chocolate for you!" Her car slowed, then it stopped completely as her window came down. I thought she was trying to possibly entrap me, because she had passed through the open fence line across the driveway; there was no way I could give her the chocolate without crossing that invisible barrier. I called out, "Dionne, you know I can't go in there!" She slowly backed up her vehicle until she was face-to-face with me on the public side of the fence, and I gave her the chocolate. She thanked me, and we wished each other a nice day. I was elated she had stopped, and that first connection had been made. I said to my friends, "Well, I know now that she'll stop for chocolate!" We thanked God that a connection had been established, even if it was over some chocolate!

Dionne's thoughts: I was thinking, should I stop or should I not? I had never stopped before for any of the protestors. But I wasn't thinking of entrapment, that was for sure. I was pretty focused on the chocolate; I'm not going to tell any stories, she snagged me with that chocolate.

Beginning of March 2019

Shiela's thoughts: Carrie and I had decided it would be nice to give baby girl presents to Dionne for her grandbaby. The two of us chose some adorable pink items to present in a gift bag. By chance, I was the one who was able to hand-deliver them to her. She stopped when she saw me holding out the present. I said, "This gift bag is from me and Carrie for your granddaughter."

Smiling, she responded with, "That is so sweet of you, thanks so much!" After that, Dionne stopped to very briefly chat with me at least once a week for the next three weeks.

Dionne's thoughts: I just thought that was real sweet. I mean, I was surprised and very appreciative.

The week prior to Easter 2019

> *Shiela texting:* Dionne, this is Shiela, the redhead outside, we brought an Easter card for you but you beat us here. What are my options to get it to you? Carrie's phone is not working so she gave me your number, I hope that is okay. I should be there at 8:30 in the morning so hopefully I'll see you to give you the card ☺

Shiela's thoughts: I was hoping she wouldn't be upset that Carrie gave me her number, but I really wanted to connect with her and get that card to her before the holiday. It just doesn't have the same impact when you receive a card after a major holiday, and I wanted to brighten her Easter.

Dionne's thoughts: When Shiela sent me a message, I'm like, "Who is Shiela? And how'd she get my number?" And then when she told me Carrie gave me her number, I was like, "Why?" And then I just thought, "Okay, whatever, it ain't no biggie," you know? I don't really care to a certain degree who has my number, because I can always change it, or just be rude, but that's not me. And it was interesting. But still in the back of my mind, I was sitting here thinking, "Why? Why she's reaching out to me?" I mean, I never really stopped before; I would wave, but...but I wanted to see what was what. Because I can be a little suspicious sometimes, but who can't? I didn't answer her initial texts. But it ended up being pretty good and working out well in the long run.

May Day 2019

> *Shiela texting:* Good evening Dionne, I apologize if I'm not spelling your name right. I just wanted to say it is a pleasure to see a smiling face driving in to the clinic. See you tomorrow morning :)

Shiela's thoughts: It can be so discouraging when there are so many people who drive in and ignore us or are rude to us, including the workers. When Dionne would come in, I at least knew she'd give us a smile and wave to us.

Dionne's thoughts: I was very surprised she spelled my name right.

June 2019

Shiela's thoughts: Dionne's son stopped to chat with me for a few minutes. He was visibly upset, telling me about a close family member who had recently passed. I felt so sad for him and Dionne, and wished to convey my condolences on their tremendous loss.

> *Shiela texting:* Good morning, I was hoping to catch you for a second on your way in because your son spoke to me yesterday about the loss of your family member. I wanted to let you know we are so, so sorry!

> *Dionne texting:* Thank you but I really don't want to talk about it.

> *Shiela texting:* That makes sense and we will respect that, just please know that you have our deepest condolences and we wish you and your family all the best and we'll pray for healing during this difficult time. I can't imagine how awful it has been. Love you!

Shiela's thoughts: I was thinking, "Oh no," that I had upset her and undone any good progress that had been made, when all I wanted to do was reach out in a loving way. I decided to give her some time before I reached out again.

Dionne's thoughts: Shiela didn't upset me. I simply don't like talking about stuff like that with anybody. I just don't deal well with it.

July 2019

Shiela's thoughts: As she was driving out of the clinic, I spoke with Demetria, Dionne's daughter, one day after she dropped off her mother. I commented, "You have the same pretty smile your mom and sweet brother have."

She replied, "Well, sometimes he's sweet."

I smiled knowingly and said, "Yeah, I have one [a brother] too."

Dionne's thoughts: She did tell me she talked to Shiela. Demi thought that Shiela was real sweet and something compelled her to stop on the way out to talk. I had never even mentioned to her that we were texting.

October-November-December 2019

Shiela's thoughts: One or more times per month I brought candy to give to Dionne and spoke to her and/or her son; they both were very friendly. I'd ask her which were her favorite types and try to bring them to her; I had a desire to interact with her as much as possible on the sidewalk.

The week before Christmas 2019

Shiela texting: Hi Dionne, we have little gifts ready for you all. Would you mind letting everybody know that we'd love for them to stop on Wednesday morning so we can hand them out to each of you. What time should we arrive to catch everybody? I made sure yours has milk chocolate :)

Dionne texting: I will be there about 8:30

Shiela texting: That sounds great, we will be ready with gifts in hand :-)

Shiela's thoughts: That was awesome to be able to hand Dionne some of the gifts (a mug individually wrapped with candy and other goodies) we had put together. Only one other worker stopped, and we had more gifts of wrapped homemade cakes and breads for her to take in as well. Now, I had never before seen this particular worker (Charlotte) smile; in fact, she usually looked angry or grimaced when driving by us into the clinic. But now, she gave me a gigantic smile, which was wonderful, lighting up her whole face. She seemed very appreciative, saying, "Oh, you have presents for me?" It warmed my heart, and made me instantly feel joyful.

Dionne's thoughts: I did tell them that Shiela wanted to hand out gifts and they said, "Whatever." After I brought the mugs in, they did use them. But they dumped the candy out on the table, so Dr. Two and I figured it was free game and ate it. One of my co-workers did say, "That was sweet of them." But a couple of the others didn't say anything.

Mid-March, 2020

Shiela's thoughts: Charlotte, the one other abortion worker who had stopped previously to take in Christmas presents, stopped for me on her way out, acting very friendly; I gave her a gift bag of soaps. I asked, "Are you heading out to get everyone lunch?"

She responded, "No, we don't take time for lunch, we just eat peanut butter and crackers."

A Few Days Later

Shiela texting: Hi, a worker told me last week you guys don't get lunch, so I thought of your staff today when I was out shopping and got you a little something to give to you or her in the morning to take in :-) I haven't tried this particular flavor yet but it looked yummy! (Here sent

119

a photo of box of "healthy" chocolate and sea-salt flavored granola-type bars.)

Dionne texting: That is nice but I don't eat them but the others may. I am a very picky eater

Shiela's thoughts: The next day I gave Dionne the box of bars in a gift bag, but also included some chocolate she liked for just her, since I knew she didn't like the bars. Little did I know that because of Coronavirus, I wouldn't be handing out any more gifts to anyone for quite a few weeks.

Dionne texting: Thank you for today

Shiela texting: You're welcome, I hope your co-workers liked the bars.

Shiela's thoughts: That was so nice that she sent me a message of thanks, even though she didn't like the bars herself.

Dionne texting: They did

Dionne's thoughts: Dr. Two really enjoyed the bars. Another worker tried them but didn't like the chocolate.

Beginning of April 2020

Shiela texting: How you doing okay? Didn't see you come in this morning, wanted to make sure you're not sick or anything

Dionne texting: I am fine, just taking a day.

Shiela texting: Oh, okay, good

Dionne texting: Thank you

Shiela texting: You're welcome, enjoy the day off! Not trying to be nosy or in your business or anything :-)

Dionne texting: It's all good

Dionne's thoughts: For her to text me when I didn't show up, it made me feel very special, it really did. Because I can get a text from Shiela and half the time my co-workers don't even call to check on me. I told them, "When I come in later than usual you should call and check up on me."

A week later

Shiela texting: I appreciate your smile and wave in the mornings :-)

Dionne texting: Same here

Dionne's thoughts: I do normally smile and wave at the other pro-lifers, but I don't stop to talk to them.

The next day

Shiela texting: Thanks, sometimes I wonder if my presence there matters

Shiela's thoughts: Well, there have been many periods of time outside the clinic when it seemed like we really weren't having that much success, because people ignored us and/or didn't keep their babies. I was feeling a little down, and again, she didn't respond.

Dionne's thoughts: That could have been a day I left my phone at home. I really do think Shiela and the others being out there makes a difference. Because it lets the ones who don't know they have options know that they do have other choices and that they are not alone.

End of April, 2020

Shiela texting: Thinking of you, hope everyone in your family is healthy and doing well!

Dionne texting: All is well and I hope all is well with you and your family

Shiela texting: Yes thanks

Dionne texting: Good to hear but you seem to be a little down to me today

Shiela texting: You mean outside the clinic or on the phone now?

Dionne texting: Outside the clinic

Shiela texting: Well, I'm honestly sad you still work there, and that the abortion numbers are rising, and I was also just plain tired this morning. :-)

Dionne texting: Oh, ok I see

Shiela texting: I like to be able to talk with you and give you presents, and this social distancing is for the birds!

Dionne texting: I know right

Shiela texting: :-(

Dionne's thoughts: It had me worried, because I thought something was wrong with Shiela. I was concerned that she didn't look her normal, cheerful self.

Shiela's thoughts: I was tired that morning, and I was also feeling down, I think because we weren't able to have as many conversations with clinic patients during the height of the Coronavirus scare, even though it seemed obvious that more women were coming for abortions. We were being careful to not get close to people, and definitely weren't handing out any materials or gifts for the time being. All I could do was give them a website to go to, or send them to a pregnancy resource center, if they asked for help. How was I supposed to make a difference in people's lives with that ministry if I couldn't give them life-saving information? But, as we remained faithful in showing up and praying, unbeknownst to me, God was faithful to continue working behind the scenes.

Middle of May 2020

Shiela's thoughts: One morning outside the abortion clinic, I asked Dionne, "Can I send you a link to an Alveda King video I just discovered about abortion?" She replied affirmatively, so I later texted her the link.[36]

> *Shiela texting:* Thanks for agreeing to watch--I wouldn't want to send you something without asking first, but you came to mind when I watched this. She's an eloquent lady that I've heard several times. See you tomorrow!

Shiela's thoughts: I was saddened that I didn't hear a response from Dionne, and thought maybe I had gone too far by sending her a pro-life video. But then, a week later she explained that she hadn't even gotten it.

Dionne's thoughts: I was having problems getting text messages; they just stopped coming in right and were black. So I eventually had to change the phone and phone number.

A week later

Shiela's thoughts: I was shocked out of my mind that next week when Dionne stopped her vehicle on the way into the clinic and gave me a small paper from a notepad with her first name and complete phone number on it. She told me, "Here, I want to give you my new phone number." As she handed me a sticky note with her name and cell number, I'm sure my mouth was agape, because I was stunned. My two friends who witnessed the exchange were also very surprised, and thanking God for what had transpired. I was just so astounded that she would do that, and I couldn't understand why. I mean, she'd had a pro-lifer bugging her on her personal cell and had a chance to get rid of me permanently. I would have never known why she had gone silent—I mean, all she had to do was not stop to talk to me anymore on that side of the fence.

> *Shiela texting*: Thanks so much for giving me your number today. Here's what I tried to send you a week ago.

> *Dionne texting:* No problem and thank you for sending me the link

> *Shiela texting*: YW ☺

Dionne's thoughts: I was really debating on whether I should give Shiela the number or not, because I didn't want her to think I was crazy or anything. I had it written on that sticky note for a week and a half, to give it to her, but then I had doubts, so I drove around with it, and then I said to myself, "Why not?" So, that morning I stopped and decided to just give it to her after all.

Beginning of June

Shiela's thoughts: Occasionally when I'd be out and about, I'd think of Dionne and wonder how she would like a certain treat. I knew she was a picky eater, and I already knew her favorite types of candies. I noticed a new type of candy one day and she came to mind.

> *Shiela texting:* Have you tried this new candy in the photo? And if so do you like it?

> *Dionne texting:* No I haven't tried it yet.

June 10, 2020

Shiela's thoughts: Dionne stopped that next morning and I gave her the new candy to try. Early in the afternoon, she texted me.

> *Dionne texting:* Thank you so very much the candy was very good

> *Shiela texting:* That's great I'm glad you liked it. Hey, how do you feel about meeting up with me after work one day? Just to chit chat about life stuff like our pets, nothing heavy. I don't do coffee, but I could do a milkshake at that fast food place down the street. If you say yes or no I won't be telling anyone about it, just my husband knows I'm asking you, and he's all for it, because everyone can use a friend right?

Shiela's thoughts: The craziest thought had become cemented into my mind that week, and I declare it came straight from the Holy Spirit, because I honestly would never have been so bold as to even think about inviting an abortion worker to meet with me over a milkshake. But first, I asked my husband, as my spiritual counselor, what he thought about the idea. He was very positive, saying, "Everyone can use a friend." He encouraged me to follow the Holy Spirit's lead in making the connection. He also thought it was a great opportunity for me, and was very surprised that she was open to it, being in the abortion industry. He remembers thinking that it was not a normal relationship, that there was a divine hand involved in bringing the two of us together, that it was ordained to happen.

> *Dionne texting:* Sounds good. I don't do coffee either but a milkshake sounds nice

Shiela's thoughts: We figured out a mutually agreeable time to meet later that week.

I was again shocked, this time that she had agreed to meet with me. I was going to be sitting down with an abortion worker;

we'd be hanging out in a public place, having a milkshake together, and my mind was whirling with disbelief.

Dionne's thoughts: The first thing I thought was "Why? Why does she really want to meet with me?" I was curious about why, so I said, "Yes."

Mid-June, 2020

Shiela's thoughts: I don't think I can adequately explain how nervous I was to meet with an abortion worker. I only knew a few small details about her, because of briefly seeing and speaking with some of her family members. I did not understand why the meeting was happening; I only knew that I was being obedient to what God was calling me to, and I was anxious to see why.

Dionne and I met at a pre-arranged fast food location, and I was honestly surprised that she wasn't taller. I had only seen her sitting up in her SUV and probably wouldn't have recognized her away from the clinic setting. We were an odd pair, at complete opposite ends of the spectrum with regards to body type/height and skin/hair coloring. After initially greeting each other, I asked her, "What flavor milkshake would you like?"

She answered, "Chocolate," so I bought us each milkshakes.

Although it was slightly annoying that the inside dining area was closed due to pandemic restrictions, the outside seating was open and the temperature was quite tolerable for a mid-June afternoon in South Carolina. I have to admit the conversation was slightly stilted at first, but we were able to keep up an easy banter. During the entire conversation we really did talk about light topics, like our children and our animals, and two whole hours just flew by. I said, "I just have three dogs for pets right now. Do you have any pets?"

She answered, "Yes, I have a cat named Doucey."

I asked, "Are you a cat person then—you don't like dogs?"

She responded, "I mean, dogs are okay; they make good pets, but I like cats. Dogs are just a little too needy for me. My brothers had some dogs growing up and I've had them. I did fall in love with one little dog that I inherited. I still talk junk about it but I loved him. But I wouldn't go out and get a dog for myself."

We actually both seemed to enjoy each other's company, and I must admit that my head was spinning in disbelief even afterwards, wondering why God was leading me in this direction. It just wasn't a normal thing for either of us to do, but God had a plan. After that meeting, Dionne typically stopped every single time to greet me and we would chat before she drove in. Conversation was easier, as we were getting to know each other better.

Dionne's thoughts: I thought she was cool beans. I honestly didn't think the conversation would go anywhere else beyond that day. I thought, *Okay, we've met, she's got the gist of who I am; I probably won't hear from her again.* I usually don't have that type of connection with anybody, to where I can just sit and talk like that, and it surprised me. Truthfully, I don't even talk that long to people I've known for years. Some people you can just feel comfortable talking to, and some you don't. I felt comfortable talking to her.

Beginning of July 2020

Shiela's thoughts: I asked her to meet with me again a few weeks later, and this time we chose a different fast-food restaurant so we could each try out a sweet dessert. We again easily chatted for a couple of hours, still pretty casual, but more in-depth about ourselves. She is a very funny lady, and she had me cracking up laughing. I had brought her some popcorn, candy and a pro-life movie that I gave to her at the end of our time together, asking her to please watch it.

Dionne's thoughts: That was interesting and I looked forward to watching it.

Dionne texting: Thank you for this afternoon ☺

Shiela texting: Hey I enjoyed it

Dionne texting: I'm glad I enjoyed it too

Shiela texting: Laughed so much!

Dionne's thoughts: That evening I texted her because I appreciated that she wanted to spend time with me again and that she gave me the movie.

End of July 2020

Shiela's thoughts: The third episode when we met was at yet another fast food restaurant, which has turned out to be our favorite location to meet ever since. She had brought her photo album that her daughter had made up for her big birthday event earlier that year, and pointed out all of her family and close friends. We discussed the pro-life movie I had given her, which she found informative, and gave me an overall positive review. The time flew by. We chatted, having an enjoyable time, and some of her relatives even stopped by. They knew who I was because I had spoken with them a couple of times when they had stopped to talk to me in the driveway. We all chatted very amicably for a few minutes, and they never questioned why she and I were there together. Believe it or not, we didn't cease conversing until a full seven hours later! It was getting late, and I had texted Robert during the evening to make sure I wasn't needed at home, but he told me to just keep doing what I was doing. Finally, I asked her, "Why did you agree to meet with me the first time?"

She answered, "It just seemed like the right thing to do. Why did you ask me to meet?"

I responded, "I just felt like the Holy Spirit was navigating me through the right steps with you. You know I couldn't have had any ulterior motive—I mean, you already knew I was a pro-lifer and didn't want you to work there!"

Dionne's thoughts: I brought the photo album because I wanted to share my special moment with her, my big day of turning 50.

Mid-August 2020

Shiela's thoughts: We met again a couple of weeks later, this time for five hours, deciding that restaurant was definitely a keeper for the rest of our meetings. Honestly, as we got to know each other, enjoyable time just always flew by. I had more time than normal because of Coronavirus, and it felt good to make a new friend. However, I still wondered, why? What was the purpose? Was there a purpose? I'm one who likes to be organized and know the plan, so I had to wholly rely on God with this relationship. And by the way, I followed the Holy Spirit's lead to keep my mouth quiet to all of my pro-life friends. They could see that obviously she would stop and chat with me, but they had no idea that we were meeting away from the clinic. One time I felt released to ask a prayer intercessor at church to pray about the situation (and it worked, because right after that was when we had our seven hour long chat), but other than that, I stayed mum. Quite honestly, that was difficult, because I wanted to shout from the rooftops that I had a new, very unlikely friend; however, I felt strongly that God didn't want me to tell anyone what was happening until His timing was right.

Around this time, the texts became more personal and will largely not be shared here. We chatted as friends about our car issues, vacations, our own ailments, major life events, like our sick kids, weddings, birthdays and anniversaries. We sent photos and discussed when we attended weddings and went on vacations. We met on average once a month throughout the summer and fall of 2020. I still occasionally texted pro-life information to her and gave gifts or other extremely helpful items when possible. That's who I am and what I do, and now she was also more than a good acquaintance. I still had no idea why we were becoming friends.

Dionne's thoughts: I was baffled. But the connection was definitely there because I just don't spend that much time with one person. Our friendship was meant to be—two opposite people. Not just opposite people, but different races, different ways of being brought up—she's just not the normal type of person I would be friends with. I don't have that many friends anyway, because I don't trust people. It's baffling to me that I trust Shiela as much as I do.

First Week of November 2020

Shiela's thoughts: One day, after spending my regular three hours in the morning outside the abortion clinic, I was headed to a church worship and prayer service, and I had the overwhelming idea come over me that it was time to write a book again. And Dionne was supposed to write it with me—this was why we connected!!! We were meant to collaborate on a book about abortion to effect a positive change in the hearts and minds of Americans. I was so excited I could barely contain myself, so at church I worshiped and praised God for orchestrating something of such a magnitude that only He could accomplish.

The next morning, I sat at the computer and typed non-stop until the book title, major points and basic outline were complete. God simply downloaded it to me in a matter of minutes. Now I just had to be obedient and present it to her.

> *Shiela texting:* If you get off early enough I have something quick I'd like to show you at the gas station down the street. The Holy Spirit knocked me over with this yesterday.

> *Dionne texting:* Okay, I will let you know when I get off work

Shiela's thoughts: I was extremely nervous to tell Dionne about my book idea. I got into her car and blurted, "I actually had this idea come to me yesterday, and I'm sure it was all from the Holy Spirit, because I wouldn't have thought of this myself, but I think the reason we connected in the first place was so we could write a book together about our friendship and how abortion hurts women. I sat down and typed all this out about the title, what it's about, and the outline, so I printed a copy for you to look over and tell me what you think." Breathless after all that, I handed her the pages to look through and waited for her to speak. Shockingly, to me, she read it quietly and then said, "That sounds like a good idea. I like it."

"Really?" I answered, "That's awesome!" I was feeling such exhilaration! Who would have thought that's why God brought us together? His timing is impeccable. It had been seven years since I'd self-published my memoir, and I had rarely written since. In fact, during my writer's workshop in 2014, the Holy Spirit led me to write that my break in writing would be for a season while I was used in other ways.

We parted on a high note, and over the weekend I began to think about what else writing a book would entail, like costs, interviews, editors, prayer partners, etc. Monday morning I sat down at the computer and created a list of items I knew we needed to discuss and see eye-to-eye on if this collaboration was going to be successful. Once again, as I sat at the computer, everything was a straight-forward download from Him, and I reached out to her again for a quick strategic meeting.

We met that afternoon for half an hour and got all the basic plans laid out seamlessly. The very first thing we had to focus on was procuring prayer partners. I had typed out a list of what we personally needed, and what our book needed to be successful in this venture, and I had in mind a few couples from my church to ask. She agreed whole-heartedly and also had someone in mind that she would reach out to. It was obvious that Someone bigger than us was orchestrating this.

Dionne's thoughts: Why would she be nervous to ask me? Why not write a book together? I want to do this because it's a good idea. I didn't take very long to consider it because I honestly thought it was a good idea to be a part of that project. Why not? I think there should be more stuff out there to educate these girls. It doesn't seem like they're being educated in their homes. Half the girls that come in there don't even feel comfortable talking to their parents. I made sure that my kids did feel comfortable talking about anything, that I'll listen and not judge them. I wish all people had that. Because when you can't go to your parents and talk, that's a problem. Anyway, God has a big part to do with this project and this relationship. He knows what He's doing. He leads, I follow.

10

Interviewing Dionne

About Protestors

SHIELA: What are your thoughts on how we came to know each other?

DIONNE: Really, I don't know; it's just weird. I never thought I would be socializing with any of the protestors out there because, especially the ones on the weekend, they can be brutal. But it ended up being, I think, the best thing that I've done. I'm glad I responded [to you] and I would like to see where it goes down the line and see what's what. And eventually, one day I will get the courage to leave the clinic behind me and venture out.

It's surprising that we've actually been texting and talking back and forth for two years. I'm surprised at that because I don't really communicate much with people nowadays... It's pretty good to have a new friend because the people I talk to now are people I've known for years. So it was nice to talk to somebody else, and you seemed like a really nice person, you did. So I replied back, and when you wanted to meet off, away from the clinic, I was surprised. I really was, I was stunned, like, "Why?" So I figured, "Why not? Let's see what's up." So I did, I agreed, and as you know, I asked you two or three times, "Why, why me?" It's crazy, but I'm glad you did reach out, and glad Carrie gave you my number. And I think we're in a good place, getting to know one another and probably will end up doing some good things, hopefully. At least, with any luck we can educate some people about life and their choices, because they do have choices.

SHIELA: What's your general impression of pro-lifers based on what you've seen outside your clinic?

DIONNE: Some are a pain in the ass. I don't really like the ones over the fence, hollering about "black lives matter," and "saving a generation." Especially when they're sounding so judgmental. They get on my nerves. Mostly it's because, well, especially on the weekend, you're hollering about how you're not judging them coming in, but that's exactly what you're doing the way you're talking to them. And they want to holler about how they're "killing those black babies in there." Really? Is that really called for?

SHIELA: Have you changed your mind at all towards pro-lifers since meeting me?

DIONNE: Yeah, some are cool. A few of them. I even wave more.

SHIELA: Do you think that my pro-life counselor friends and I make a difference, good or bad?

DIONNE: I think they do good, honestly. I really do. Because they don't try to tell them what they should and shouldn't do; giving them options, coming at them with a different approach, which makes them want to listen to what they have to say. So I think they're doing a good service out there.

SHIELA: Different pro-lifers have different methods of expressing themselves to the patients coming in; how do you think their approach matters?

DIONNE: It matters a lot because the ones that are being obnoxious are actually helping the patients to make up their minds even more to have the abortion. They feel like they're being judged, and it's a more harsh approach the way they're doing it. If they took a different approach to be more sympathetic, then they would get better results, to really help people think about their choice. But if you're just going to throw out words to accuse them of killing their generation-to-be, calling out "black lives matter,"…no, I think all lives matter; it doesn't have anything to do with race; but they play that race card a lot.

SHIELA: What about when they play worship music and read from the Bible?

DIONNE: I don't have a problem with that, but it doesn't have to be that loud. It's bad enough we have to hear it when we get out of our cars, but when we're inside with the doors closed we can still hear it. Some of that music is really nice, though.

SHIELA: People often honk in support of us pro-lifers outside the clinic. Can you hear the honks from the cars driving by on the street?

DIONNE: We hear the honking, especially when people are out there holding the "Honk for Life" signs. I've even honked when I've driven by on my days off.

SHIELA: Really? Why?

DIONNE: To save a life. I like that "Honk for Life" sign. I like to hear the honking; it lets me know somebody cares about a life.

SHIELA: Do patients complain about the pro-life protestors outside?

DIONNE: Not much during the week. The ones that patients complain about are the ones during the weekend and the ones up at the top of the fence, the loud ones. They get quite irritated with those men. They don't complain about the ones at the entrance where they drive in. If we [employees] need to drive out to leave, we can't even see when they block our view. That's very dangerous.

SHIELA: Do patients ever tell you if they stopped to talk to us?

DIONNE: No, they don't mention it at all. The rest of the office staff tell everyone on the phone not to stop to talk to the [pro-life] protestors, but I never tell them that.

SHIELA: What do you think about the pro-abortion counter-protestors?

DIONNE: When the other ones [pro-aborts] are out there, they really get on my nerve and I wish the office manager had never told them they could come to park in our lot in the first place. But they do have a right to voice their opinion; however, when she gave them the right of where they could park, it's like they're saying they're a part of us. They shouldn't be on our property because they're protestors too. Even though it's "for abortion" but pro-testing's not what we're really about; if we wanted people to protest for us, we'd be out there ourselves. They can be just as obnoxious as the others [pro-lifers], if not more. The atmosphere seems to be worse when they're out there. Even though, in their mind, they think they're helping the situation, they're not.

Various Abortion Topics

SHIELA: What have you seen to be women's top five reasons for having abortions?

DIONNE: One-night stand. Either they were raped, or they cheated on their husband, so they don't know whose it is, and they're going to abort because they don't want their husbands to find out. And some, because they don't want the baby, and some, basically, because they don't think it's the right time in their life.

SHIELA: That's a lot of one-night stands.

DIONNE: Yep, because a pretty big part of our clientele are the strippers. And of course, they go home with some of the guys, so....

SHIELA: From what I've seen, more women at your clinic take the pill versus having surgery; why is that?

DIONNE: They have it in their mind they're taking a pill so they're not having an abortion, and then the pill is cheaper.

SHIELA: So they're justifying it in their minds and also trying to save a hundred bucks? What percentage would you guestimate choose the pill?

DIONNE: Yep. It's probably over two-thirds that go in for the pill instead of surgery.

SHIELA: Why is it disproportionately minorities that come for abortions?

DIONNE: Because they let their husbands tell them what to do. Most of them that come in there are married. Their husband speaks for them.

SHIELA: But because of Coronavirus restrictions the husbands usually aren't allowed inside the clinic if she speaks English though, are they?

DIONNE: They don't come in, but she still has to at least nod or say yes. She has to agree to it. And I know the only reason she is agreeing is because she has to go home with that man and we don't.

SHIELA: What is your opinion of the big push for telehealth abortions—women taking RU-486 via mail-order with no doctor involved, or just a doctor over a webcam?

DIONNE: For real? I hadn't even heard about that. I don't think that's a good idea. I don't even like Plan B being over-the-counter. I don't think taking the [abortion] pill without being checked by a doctor is safe. No, I don't think that's good. Face-to-face. And the main reason I don't think the abortion pill being over-the-counter is safe is because we've had more than a handful of girls that come in, they get a positive pregnancy test, but they're not actually pregnant. But then they get mad at us because we won't give them the pill.

Well, you're not pregnant! And if they do that at home and they can get this over the counter, if they get a positive pregnancy test, they're going to take this pill anyway, because in their mind they're pregnant when half of them are not. Because anything can throw off a pregnancy test, if you're stressed or whatever, you can get a false positive. And a lot of them get a false positive and want to argue with us, but we say, "You're not pregnant; we're not going to give you the pill." A woman will say, "But I know I'm pregnant, I know I am." We have to tell her, "Look, we did an ultrasound, then we ran more than one pregnancy test, and you're not pregnant." And another thing is, they don't know how far along they are for sure without the ultrasound. They shouldn't be taking the pill past ten weeks.

SHIELA: So, then, women who aren't pregnant or are too far along will be taking this with a wrong diagnosis.

DIONNE: Yes! And the side-effects like bleeding could be dangerous!

SHIELA: How do you feel about late-term abortions and do you think you would work there if they did them?

DIONNE: I don't like the idea of abortions up to 24 weeks or beyond; at the moment I don't know if I would still be working there. But I do believe if they were doing them up to 24 or beyond in the beginning I would probably have never been working there.

SHIELA: How do you feel about U.S. taxpayers funding abortions abroad? In other countries?

DIONNE: I think that's crazy. I think that's just downright crazy. Our taxpayers are paying enough and we shouldn't have to pay for that. In other countries, NO!

SHIELA: Now, you know, in Oregon, if you're a taxpayer, you're paying for state-funded abortions; they're all free on demand in Oregon. For ANY reason, free on demand.

DIONNE: No-no-no, I don't agree with that, no, uh-uh, no, that's crazy!

SHIELA: I've talked to women outside the clinic who told me they or their friends came for botched abortions and the doctors here saved their lives recently or even decades ago. I've gotten the impression that these two doctors are good at what they do. You've seen botched abortions and seen these doctors save lives?

DIONNE: Yep. A handful of times. You'd be surprised at some of the problems. I don't know where they went for the botched abortions, but they've come completely covered in blood and the doctors have helped them.

SHIELA: Ambulances go by all the time, and people ask me frequently, "Have you ever seen an ambulance go in here?" And I say, "No, they seem to be quite good at their profession."

DIONNE: Yeah, that's a rarity.

SHIELA: One main reason people say we should have legalized abortions is because of women who do illegal ones, or back-alley type abortions, have you seen that happen often? I know that a patient told me she tried to abort her own baby years ago and that Dr. One saved her life, so she's remained his patient for decades.

DIONNE: Yes, actually, we've had a couple that have had illegal abortions. Sometimes they do it themselves and then you've got some shade-trees like you do with mechanics. You've got some folks who do it on the side, but they aren't supposed to.

SHIELA: What do you think is the solution to abortion? Is there one?

DIONNE: I don't really think there is one. Because even if it wasn't legal, they're still going to find a way to abort it.

Her Personal Views of Abortion

SHIELA: What is your opinion of abortion?

DIONNE: Me personally, I never thought a person should have an abortion, but some times when I do watch or catch the news and hear about some of these crazy people that kill their kids or beat them, then yeah, maybe they should have had an abortion, because apparently they didn't want their child anyway, if you're going to treat them like that. I'd rather for you to have aborted than to beat that child, because she didn't ask to be in this world.

SHIELA: Have you ever felt that someone should have an abortion?

DIONNE: No, I've never felt that.

SHIELA: No? You haven't heard a reason good enough?

DIONNE: No, I haven't heard a reason.

SHIELA: That's pretty huge, you know that?

DIONNE: Because there is no reason!

SHIELA: Do you know how pro-life that sounds?

DIONNE: Huh?

SHIELA: Do you know how pro-life that sounds? And, you're pro-choice, but you have never seen—you've worked there all these years!

DIONNE: No, there's no excuse.

SHIELA: And how many thousands...you've participated in thousands, and heard thousands of stories....

DIONNE: Uh-huh, and there's still no excuse.

SHIELA: And you've still never heard an excuse good enough?

DIONNE: No

SHIELA: Wow. Well, okay, tell me this, do you feel like you can understand why women do it?

DIONNE: To a certain degree.

SHIELA: Because I feel like I do—I talk out there to them, and I realize they think they're in a certain circumstance—and this is their only choice—

DIONNE: —right, they feel like it's their only choice because they don't know the other options.

SHIELA: Uh-huh, and there are other options, but I can totally understand why they're doing it.

DIONNE: To a certain degree

SHIELA: Because of how much they know, or what they don't know

DIONNE: Or what they choose to know

SHIELA: I understand, and that's why I don't judge them. I want to educate them, because I feel like they don't know, and they might hopefully make a different choice if they do.

DIONNE: And some of them do, and they still make that choice.

SHIELA: Yeah. They do, because we tell them. We tell them about their options; they might not believe us, or they're not willing to—

DIONNE: They don't want to go through it [having the baby].

SHIELA: Yeah. It's sad.

DIONNE: But at the end of the day, it's their decision. They're the one who's got to live with it, not me.

SHIELA: Are peoples' reasons usually valid or just excuses in your opinion?

DIONNE: Excuses.

SHIELA: I'm in shock still—I'm surprised that you say you can't see valid reasons for women that come in.

DIONNE: Because there is not one. There is not one. Not ONE!

SHIELA: Why do you think so many women come for abortions?

DIONNE: 'Cause they think it's better than to have to raise them for 18 years. And that's the sad truth.

SHIELA: You already said cases of rape happen often; that's sad. Is it like cases of date rape, or people they don't even know?

DIONNE: It is sad; no, it's incest, basically.

SHIELA: So they know the people.

DIONNE: Yeah! Some dude the single mother has brought into the home. When you've got kids like that, you don't bring a man in to live with you, or to visit, regardless. You're asking for trouble. Why would you bring a man that you don't even really know? And yeah, you've got some uncles that do it, daddies that do it.

SHIELA: But still, in none of those cases, you still don't think abortion is right?

DIONNE: I just, I just don't. You know, even though I would hate for a 12 or 13 year old to have to go through anything like that, but it's still no reason to abort a child. They didn't ask for it.

SHIELA: Works for me. How do you know it's not good for women to have abortions if they have no reactions when they come back and don't talk to you about it?

DIONNE: I don't really think it's that bad; I don't see how it hurts them. It doesn't affect if they want to have kids along the line; it doesn't affect that.

SHIELA: It can.

DIONNE: But it doesn't.

SHIELA: No, I mean, some people it does. Women can have a uterus so scarred that it's difficult or impossible for them to have children.

DIONNE: I haven't come across any.

SHIELA: Maybe not with your doctors, because they're good at what they do.

DIONNE: Oh, yeah, they are. But I, firsthand, I don't see how it hurts them. Now, they may have some mental problems later 'cause they were forced to do it, but the ones that actually have in their minds this is what they want to do, no.

SHIELA: But you see them crying when they're leaving, don't you? Or do they wait until they get into the car? Because we see them bawling on the way out, and then they come in for their checkups or even when they're coming in the first place, we see them bawling and in emotional huge struggles all the time.

DIONNE: Let me tell you—not when they leave. It's usually after we've walked them to the car, and the guy or whoever is picking them up, "How you doing?" That's when they want to bawl. But emotion, no. Half of them, while they're there, in recovery, they're laughing and talking, playing on their phone, asking us questions, "How soon can I have sex again? Can I have a drink when I get home?" Those are the main questions they ask when they're in recovery. That's where their mindset is.

SHIELA: Are there any positives to abortion? Because you've said you can't think of a reason why they should have one. Other than it keeps you employed, for NOW? (Dionne laughs) Hopefully not much longer.

DIONNE: I really can't think of any

SHIELA: What goes through your mind when you take care of the remains, or specimen, as you say?

DIONNE: That's why I say I'm mixed about it being a baby because of what I see. Yes, some of them are, some are not. Because on some of them that are early, it's just like you're looking at an egg yolk under a microscope to where you can see the little sack and yolk. That's what most of them look like. Except for the ones that are further along.

SHIELA: The smaller size fetuses go through the small tube that I'm sure smashes them to unrecognizable, bloody "clots" you've described because they're still so soft, but if you saw them formed instead, I'm just curious, would that make a difference in how you think about them at that gestational age?

DIONNE: No, it doesn't matter, one way or the other.

SHIELA: Watching the medical waste truck leave just about makes me physically ill and feel like I want to vomit; I'm glad I'm hardly ever there that day it comes every other week.

DIONNE: Yes, it came today.

SHIELA: Do you have any thoughts about when it comes and goes? You're the one giving it to him.

DIONNE: I don't know. It might be why, not that I'm doing it on purpose, but normally I'm late on that day. So he's gone by the time I get there.

SHIELA: But when he comes, don't you have to give it to him?

DIONNE: No, any of the others can get it out of the freezer to give to him.

SHIELA: They take the bag from the freezer and seal it and give him the bag?

DIONNE: Yes, he puts it in his bin and seals it and leaves.

More Personal Questions

SHIELA: Tell me about your Christian background and beliefs, growing up in church. Has the Holy Spirit played a part in how you choose what you do in life?

DIONNE: I was christened when I was a baby and then I did get re-baptized when I was around 20 before my first baby was born. We are Methodists and Baptists. My belief—it's the main part. It's the center of my world. Even though I know it probably doesn't go with anyone else's, but it's mine. I thank Him every morning and every night. I believe in the Holy Spirit.

SHIELA: How do you reconcile working in an abortion clinic and being a Christian?

DIONNE: Like I say, I say my prayers every night, "Forgive me for my sins," and every day.

SHIELA: Do you think abortion is a sin?

DIONNE: Yeah and no.

SHIELA: Yeah and no? Explain please.

DIONNE: Yeah, to a certain degree, because you are taking a life, and, "thou shalt not kill."

SHIELA: I asked a 17-year-old, that I had talked to with her mom on the way in to the clinic, why she changed her mind. And she said, "Thou shalt not kill." So, in that regard, it is a sin.

DIONNE: Yes.

SHIELA: Well, then, how is it not a sin? I mean, because it either is a sin or it isn't, right?

DIONNE: Because. I'm kind of flip-floppy about it because to a certain degree, yeah, it is a fetus, and to a certain degree, it's not. It's not developed. I have mixed feelings about it.

SHIELA: But you know it's a life.

DIONNE: To a certain degree. Because it's got a heartbeat but it hasn't taken a breath out. So I have mixed feelings about that one.

SHIELA: Okay. What do you think God thinks about abortion?

DIONNE: Now, that's a hard one. Because...I don't know. I really don't know. Because if it goes back to, thou shalt not kill, but you gave them the education for this. It's just as well your fault as anyone else's, so I don't know, I'm torn between that.

SHIELA: (Very confused) Wait—who...gave—what?

DIONNE: (Dionne laughing) God. I mean, You (God) gave them the ability to be able to do this.

SHIELA: To abort?

DIONNE: The ability, yes. I mean even though He might not have wanted them to—

SHIELA: (Interrupting) God gave who, the doctors?

DIONNE: The doctors. Even though He probably didn't give them that ability to do it in that way, yeah, I made you a doctor or whatever, gave you the knowledge to become a doctor, but how you chose to use it is totally up to you. But you gave them the skills. I don't know. I'm mixed on that one.

SHIELA: Speaking of the doctors, what do you think your co-workers will say about you doing this project?

DIONNE: Probably nothing, or, "Why didn't you ask me? I could have given you some input," or something along those lines, knowing them.

SHIELA: Why wouldn't you want to use a pseudonym to write this? You're not worried about the doctors getting angry at you?

DIONNE: No, I hadn't even thought about it. I'd say, "Before you judge, read the book."

SHIELA: What does your family think about you doing this?

DIONNE: They don't care, but my son thought he should be mentioned more.

SHIELA: What would you say to other abortion workers?

DIONNE: What do you mean?

SHIELA: Well, you're an abortion worker, so do you think that is a job that other people should go in to? Or if they are, should they stay an abortion worker?

DIONNE: I wouldn't convince anybody to become one, no! No, I'm not out here, "Come work here!" No! There's other things out there you could do.

SHIELA: Yeah, but there's a reason why you're not saying, you know, "This is a great thing to come do!"

DIONNE: No, I wouldn't tell anyone that.

SHIELA: Why not?

DIONNE: It's just nothing I would advertise. A lot of people who know me don't even know what I do for a living. All they know is that I work at a private clinic. And I leave it at that.

SHIELA: So you don't advertise it.

DIONNE: No!

SHIELA: What have been reactions from people who have found out?

DIONNE: The crazy thing is, the ones that have found out, it's because they walked their tails through that door. They say, "Oh, I didn't know you worked here."

SHIELA: Do people from church know or care where you work?

DIONNE: Yeah, now my pastor does know. I don't socialize with too many people in my church, but my pastor does know.

SHIELA: What's she think about it? Does she care? Not care?

DIONNE: I mean, she wished I worked somewhere else, but…it pays the bills.

SHIELA: Why does your daughter work at the clinic also?

DIONNE: I get some folks that ask me how I can have my daughter working there. It's not like I said, "Demi, I want you to come and work there." Every time my daughter talks about working there full-time, I say, "No, you've got a full-time job, this is not where I want you, not here; when you get things situated financially to do what you want to do, maybe you can get out of this too." Because originally it was just to help out in a bind. My daughter came in when we lost a co-worker and needed help up front, but I knew it wasn't going to be anything permanent for her. So it was just something to get her an extra boost to get her car and stuff paid off. She just comes in occasionally up to two days, but she's working on starting her business and I'm behind that 100%, because eventually she'll be doing that full-time. She's still young and she can still do it.

SHIELA: We've sort of tip-toed around this question. How does it make you feel working there?

DIONNE: I don't think about it, so I can't really answer that question.

SHIELA: Okay, so, you're compartmentalizing and putting aside the fact that....

DIONNE: It's just a job, yeah, I don't think about it. When I walk through that door in the morning, I'm happy that I'm up and about, but yeah, it's just like any other job.

SHIELA: You've told me if you had to do it again you would go back to work at the clinic, but you've also said you would not do it again, so which is it really?

DIONNE: Well, I said I would because of the women that I've helped change their minds when they were undecided. When they asked me what I would do and I told them, so that's been nice to see they didn't go through with it. That made me feel good that they kept their babies.

SHIELA: Do you see yourself continuing to work at the clinic?

DIONNE: Actually, I do see myself leaving the clinic. When, I'm not really sure, because like I said, it's very difficult for me. I'm 50 years old, and change...I mean, because a lot of people aren't going to hire someone in their 50's. But who knows what the future may hold. I may be at the beach doing something else, but I do think when I leave the clinic I will be leaving Greenville also; but who knows? Maybe I'll stay in Greenville for a while and just leave the clinic.

SHIELA: What is an important message you want people to take away from this book?

DIONNE: Kids need to know that they would have the support of their family, and they need to be educated on their choices if they do become pregnant. So many more mothers would choose life if they only knew what was out there to help them.

Kindness should begin at home.

1 Timothy 5:4

Part Five

Conclusions About the Fence

11

Reflections

Try always to be led along together by the Holy Spirit and be at peace with one another.

Ephesians 4:3

Be gentle and ready to forgive; never hold grudges. Remember the Lord forgave you, so you must forgive others. Let love guide your life and always be thankful.

Colossians 3:13

A further reason for forgiveness is to keep from being outsmarted by Satan, for we know what he is trying to do.

2 Corinthians 2:11

Shiela writing:

About Forgiveness

Soon after I became more involved with the pro-life ministry in the fall of 2018, Satan stirred up problems in my family life, when Robert and I had a major breakdown in our marriage. Thankfully, we were able to go to Gene Wagstaff at Word of God Counseling,[37] who is a great local marriage counselor, focused on forgiveness towards all. Satan, who tries to kill, steal, and destroy, especially loves to distract those who are called to mission work; however, God used this event for His good, as we were actually able to learn a lot about forgiveness. We not only healed our marriage, but were able to learn to forgive so many others in our lives. The whole experience overall helped me be an even better sidewalk counselor and mentor to others, explaining how we have to forgive every person of everything we perceive they have done to wrong us, every single day. Whether it's someone who drives by giving us an obscene finger gesture, a pro-abort protestor screaming in our face, or an abortionist honking angrily at us, we still have a duty to forgive them. That doesn't mean condoning what they do but it does mean loving them where they're at right now. God loves them as much as He loves you or me, and if we hold animosity in our hearts towards others, Satan will use that against us in the court of heaven. Forgiving others at all times is definitely easier said than done, and it takes practice, but it's so worth it!

Gene spoke to some of us at a pro-life training seminar and gave us excellent advice on how to deal with angry, aggressive pro-choice activists, abortion workers, or anyone else who opposes our ministry:

Their truth doesn't match our truth, so there's opposition. We know our identity in Christ, and that we are made in God's image, but they don't know who they are or what they're doing. It's true we have righteous anger towards them, but coming against them emotionally doesn't work. Our fight is against the spiritual forces of evil.

Why do they believe the way they do? We have a different input into our minds, and their strongholds can be demolished if we know how to do spiritual warfare. Recognize that the fight isn't against them, because they are only flesh and blood. They are not the enemy; they don't know who they were created to be, which is to be a son or daughter of God. They don't have that thought process because they don't yet know who they are. We are submitted to the Holy Spirit; they aren't. The devil wants you to accuse them, but we need to go to God, be strong, and resist the devil. He accuses us in the courtroom of heaven. Those bad thoughts from the devil are the ones we need to take captive.

There is power in the spoken word, and one day we will have to give account for every careless word we utter. Instead of calling the abortion workers "baby-killers," bless them to give life and forgive them to take those bad thoughts captive. Referring to Mark 11:23 (about having the faith to move a mountain), the clinic is our "mountain," and we need to forgive them so that God will listen to us and forgive us. Our objective is for them to know who they are. Say, "I bless you in your destiny as a child of God."

How do we go to war? Forgive them, or He doesn't even hear us. Forgive the offense against them. We've all been called to suffer for doing nothing wrong and to bless our enemy. We're called to take sin on us. Our Heavenly Father knows we're innocent, but when we try to convince others of our innocence, it's just spiritual idolatry. By our sufferings they can be healed: go to the Father and bless them to be free of these lies they hold to be truth. Forgive them and bless them until we break through. 1 Peter 3:8 (NIV): "Finally, all of you, be like-minded, be sympathetic, love one another, be compassionate and humble." Be sad, not mad. Jesus wasn't mad on the cross. Petition God, "I ask you to loosen Satan's hold over them and that they would know their true destiny in You."

About Hormonal Birth Control and Natural Family Planning

I decided to attend my first March for Life in Washington, D.C., trying to do my part to raise awareness that abortion hurts women. We traveled up the day before, on January 17, 2019. As it happened, I rode up and back on a bus with a Catholic group from my area. I sat next to my friend, Valerie Baronkin, who has been a local pro-life leader for some time. She explained to me how hormonal birth control can actually be abortifacient, which was something I had never heard before. I asked, "So, I'm fairly new to learning about this whole topic, can you explain to me why Catholics are so against hormonal birth control?"

She answered, "Did you know that hormonal birth control is an abortifacient, meaning the pill can cause an abortion?"

I replied, "No, I had no idea, and I was on them for several years after we got married." This was a brand-new revelation for me, and I wanted to know more.

She went on to further educate me, "These drugs are used to prevent pregnancy by trying to stop ovulation, but if ovulation occurs and a child is conceived, there is another part of the drug that will prevent implantation of a baby, therefore causing a chemical abortion. When I was young, I took hormonal birth control too. Since I found Jesus and the truth about these pills, I pray I was not responsible for killing my child while taking these drugs. There are other problems with hormonal birth control. There is a direct link between taking these pills and breast cancer. My close friend believes her breast cancer, which is now metastatic cancer, was caused by the high estrogen birth control she took so many years ago. She has been disabled for over 25 years with three rounds of chemotherapy and radiation and is currently on a low dose of chemo for the rest of her life. By the grace of God, she is alive to see her grand-children.

"Birth control pills are identified as a first class carcinogen that causes cancer, but no one talks about that.[38] No one talks about the fact that birth control also causes strokes and heart attacks. These warnings are labeled on the box. Young girls that are otherwise healthy are having strokes and no one is relating the cause to their birth control. I have a friend that I was talking to about her heart attack, and she related that it was because of stress. Our conversation went on to various other areas and she said she was on a certain type of birth control. I then blurted out, 'That's what caused your heart attack!' She said she did not realize, and she would talk to her doctor about it. It's interesting that not long after, that particular brand of birth control was taken off the market, since many women were having similar problems. But the problem is with all artificial birth control. It is strange how this friend, like many other women, exercises regularly, eats healthy and tries to live a healthy life but puts these artificial hormone chemicals into her body daily.

"Some people use abortion as a backup for failed contraception. In fact, this is why over 50% of abortions occur.[39] The good news is there is a natural way that couples can use to avoid or achieve pregnancy called Natural Family Planning (NFP). NFP works with a woman's natural cycle without drugs or harmful side effects. Everything God creates is good and so is the sexual union. God created sexual union with two aspects, unitive and the pro-creative. He made these aspects to work together. If you have one without the other, it is void of God's graces because we are distorting His gift. NFP is a scientific method where the couple can work together with the natural cycles of a woman's fertility to prevent pregnancy. Of course, God's command is to be fruitful and multiply but sometimes the couple is not in a position to have another child.

"I have a couple young friends who had fertility problems and wanted to have children. They worked with Natural Family Planning practitioners and doctors to find and correct the underlying cause of their fertility problems. They were able to get pregnant and have some very beautiful children. NFP has been shown to have double or even triple the success rate than in vitro fertilization (IVF) in achieving a pregnancy.[40] IVF is very expensive, costing tens of thousands of dollars. During IVF, the doctors give women artificial hormones, and the baby is created outside the sexual union in a sterile petri dish. The doctors grade the embryos and only implant the best ones. Is this part of the eugenics movements, where only the best survive? If too many babies are implanted and survive in the womb, the doctors will perform a selective reduction, which is a nice way of saying they abort weaker babies as multiple births are riskier for the mother. We need to educate women there are better choices. God has provided us with wonderful, natural ways for our precious gift of fertility and the world needs to know."

There was further information on these topics at the pro-life expo that I visited in D.C. in the morning before the march began; it had information booths with brochures that linked hormonal birth control to all sorts of physical problems for women, and offered Natural Family Planning (NFP) methods instead.

I had heard of this from Carrie also, as it is her passion that women be completely natural with everything that affects their bodies.

Carrie writing:

My favorite information to give out on the sidewalk outside the abortion facility is information on Natural Family Planning. About one quarter of the clients who enter the abortion facility are going for various forms of artificial birth control to avoid pregnancy or remediate health conditions or, less frequently, are seeking help with getting pregnant. When they tell me that is why they are there, I am thrilled to tell them about NFP to let them know they have the option to plan their family naturally and get help for their health without chemicals or devices or treatments that can be harmful to their bodies, their emotions, their relationships, and the environment, and can additionally be abortifacient. I made a flyer about NFP that I share with them.[41]

NFP methods are now as efficacious medically to avoid pregnancy as artificial means, and are more efficacious to achieve pregnancy than artificial fertility treatments. Plus they are positive and healthy. NFP allows women and men to learn so much about their bodies and to find natural solutions to other reproductive health conditions, not just to avoidance and achievement of pregnancy. It is so empowering and awe-inspiring for women and men to understand the beauty and workings of their own and each other's bodies better.

Natural Family Planning cultivates self-respect, and in a relationship, it cultivates mutual respect, communication, equality, prayer, and a closer emotional and spiritual bond. It gives a couple the opportunities to seek the Lord together, rely on the fruit of the Holy Spirit, and find other ways to love each other if they choose to abstain during times of fertility. It restores the integrity of our bodies and the definition of our sexuality. It allows teens to prepare for future marriage by learning to respect themselves for who they are and by knowing that each partner in a relationship can respect and be respected as freely, wholly, and naturally themselves. Young people and all people need to know they can be themselves and they are beautiful just as they are, just as God made them!

This is the message of Natural Family Planning! We can be Free, Whole and Natural - exactly who we are, and We are Beautiful just as we are!! My heart's desire is for all people to hear this NFP message and to know the many benefits NFP provides physically, emotionally, and spiritually for individuals and couples. I hope it can spread like wildfire through the church and across our society. It avails those of us on each side of the abortion debate to come together under a banner that fosters self-respect, respect between men and women, and respect for the environment.

Pro-life and pro-choice women and men can all agree that methods that preserve our health and the environment and improve our relationships are preferable to those that don't. Realizing these beautiful benefits is revolutionary and freeing and restores our true identities! Natural Family Planning is therefore a big part of the solution to abortion, sex trafficking, divorce, abuse, gender confusion, and all the sexual and relational brokenness in our world. NFP is a wonderful, positive, and sadly underutilized opportunity to bring healing, truth, freedom, and hope to so many and to reverse trends that are destroying lives and grieving our Creator. May we grasp and claim our own beauty and the many natural gifts our Creator has given us! There are great websites where you can learn more.[42]

About Abortion Hurting Women

Since as many as 50% of post-abortive women hide their previous abortions from interviewers, researchers have to use "record based studies that do not rely on surveys of women but instead look directly at their medical records to assess their post abortion symptoms."[43] One such study from Finland, using government records from their government health care system that covers all health care costs including abortion, revealed that women who had an abortion "were three times more likely to commit suicide within a year of their abortion than women in the general population, and more than six times likely to commit suicide than women who carried their pregnancy to term."[44]

Another study from California examined the death records of low-income women. "Compared to women who delivered, those who aborted were 154 percent more likely to die from suicide and 82 percent more likely to die from accidents (which may be related to suicidal behavior). The higher suicide rates were most pronounced in the first four years following the pregnancy outcome."[45]

In 1989 the *Los Angeles Times* surveyed 3,583 people, discovering that 56% of women admitted to a sense of guilt after abortion and 26% regretted choosing abortion.[46]

At the end of the March for Life 2019, I listened over an hour to the 35 moving "Silent No More" testimonies presented at the base of the steps of the Supreme Court of the United States. These brave men and women spoke publicly of their abortion stories; some were parents who had themselves lost children to abortion, and some were friends or relatives who regretted assisting someone else having an abortion. Their stories were poignant—they were exposing the truth that abortion hurts not only the mother, but everyone else involved as well. I personally hadn't heard that shared anywhere before, and I felt a need to write about it to educate others. Since I had become more vocal online about my experiences at the clinic, people started telling me their own abortion stories. I realized the stories were so emotionally charged and compelling against abortion that they needed to be shared with the women going into the clinic. This became a tri-fold brochure that I hand out when I am able. Eight stories are of women who had an abortion, while four did not. I believe God inspired the brochure because it all came flooding together very quickly to completion, and it is a game-changer when people read it.[47]

For example, once a Hispanic couple read my abortion stories tri-fold after they drove into the clinic and came out an hour later; the woman opened the brochure and asked me, "Is this really true?"

I said, "Yes, I wrote it—those are friends of mine who told me their stories."

She said, "Well, I changed my mind after I read it."

Portions of Pro-Life Brochure:
"You're Here for an Abortion—How Will Your Story End?"
(compiled and written by Shiela Miller)

"I WAS IN AN ABUSIVE RELATIONSHIP THE FIRST TWO TIMES I HAD AN ABORTION AT AGE 26. Now, years later I have two adult and two teenage children that I love very much, but every day I am filled with guilt, grief, and remorse for those I lost. Please don't make the same choice I did." —Aniyah P.

"I DIDN'T TELL MY PARENTS I WAS PREGNANT, AND ALL OF MY FRIENDS WERE VERY SUPPORTIVE OF WHATEVER CHOICE I DECIDED TO MAKE. Sadly, I drove to this very clinic and decided to have an abortion; since then, I've had to go through healing counseling because it was so emotionally traumatic. There wasn't a single person who told me I shouldn't do it. If you, Shiela, had just been outside when I went, I would have changed my mind and not gone through with it. I want to tell others to please make a better choice than I did." —Ella T.

"MY NIECE WAS IN THE 9TH GRADE WHEN HER PARENTS FORCED HER TO HAVE AN ABORTION. Afterwards, her nerves were shot. She went through years of therapy for depression—she cried so much! I don't feel any parent should force their child to go through that, because I saw the outcome firsthand. Don't allow yourself to be forced into an abortion, because you are the one who has to live with the consequences." —Anna W.

"I WAS 20 YEARS OLD WHEN I FOUND OUT I WAS PREGNANT. I had just ended a strained relationship with my boyfriend weeks before and moved out of state. I was devastated. In my mind, there were no other options. I wish someone had informed me otherwise. I had an abortion and spent a solid 16 years in a downward spiral of emotional, mental, and spiritual darkness, which led to a repeated cycle of poor and painful life decisions. Glory to God, I am finally healing, though I will never forget. I wish I had known then what I know now. I encourage you to recognize there IS a precious life inside of you, no matter how far along, and to choose one of the numerous other options for you and your baby." —Mary E.

"MY SISTER WAS MARRIED WITH TWO CHILDREN, AND THEY DECIDED TO ABORT THEIR THIRD. They didn't think it was best financially at the time. Her life spiraled out of control as she went through depression and was diagnosed as bipolar. They argued, blaming each other for the decision, and eventually divorced. I know she feels she should have listened to her motherly instinct and would want you to listen as well." —Latoya G.

"AFTER MY SISTER'S ABORTION, SHE DECIDED TO GET PREGNANT AGAIN AND HAVE ANOTHER BABY TO HELP HER 'RECOVER'. However, it didn't work and she was still so traumatized that she committed suicide, orphaning her 18-month-old daughter." —Linda R.

"I WAS RAISING A VERY YOUNG CHILD WHEN I FOUND OUT I WAS ALREADY PREGNANT A SECOND TIME. I decided to have an abortion, but the next time I was pregnant and gave birth, it was to a set of beautiful twins. I have always been heartsick wondering if I aborted not just one, but multiple babies. I wish someone had told me beforehand how emotionally painful abortion is to a woman. Please heed this warning and choose to leave the abortion clinic right now so you don't live with questions and regrets like me for the rest of your life." —Josefina M.

"AT AGE 64, I STILL REGRET MY DECISION FROM 47 YEARS AGO. You see, I became pregnant right before starting my freshman year of college. I knew I couldn't trust my boyfriend to take care of me, let alone a baby. I just couldn't stand the thought of the embarrassment and shame, and my parents would be devastated. He said he'd do whatever, so I chose an abortion. After the procedure, my first thought was, 'I killed my baby.' I quickly shoved aside that thought and all the feelings that went with it, and told myself, 'I have to go home and forget this ever happened.' But I couldn't forget. Every time I saw a baby or a pregnant woman, I remembered. I fell into a deep depression and eventually even became suicidal, requiring much counseling. No one tells you how you'll feel if you choose abortion. I'm telling you now, please choose life over death." —Kathy L.

Janet writing:

I chose abortion years ago because it was a hard time for me. The guy I was with was abusive, and I just couldn't deal with life. Abortion seemed like the way out. The day I had my abortion, I went into a place that was cold and dark— just sadness, no feeling of life. When it was time for my procedure, they had me sedated but I was still very aware of what was happening to me. No one asked me at all if I wanted to see my ultrasound. I remember during the proce-dure I experienced tremendous cramping and as I felt my unborn baby being ripped from my body, I knew my life would be forever changed. A part of me died that day with my baby. I felt deep emptiness in me where there was once life. I felt immediate regret and guilt and a sense that I had just sinned against God. The emotional side of this was so devastating. I just wanted to end it all because I knew I could never undo the horrible act I just committed, and that was taking the life of my own flesh and blood. My heart started growing hard that day.

If I had not been in the church I was in at the time, believing that committing suicide would send me straight to hell, I would have definitely taken my own life. That was all that saved me, and I had to go on.

I had been feeling for some time that God was pulling me towards volunteering outside the abortion clinic. When I heard that Shiela ministered there on a regular basis, I asked her for the information and received training also. And not long after, I decided to take a six-week post-abortive healing class through a pregnancy resource center.

First starting the class you have to make sure you've repented and ask forgiveness so you can start the class out right, communicating with the Lord. Then you have to believe that the Lord has forgiven you. Then you have to ask the Lord to show you all the people that you have unforgiveness toward. I thought at first it was just me; then I thought about it and asked Him to show me, and I realized I put blame on everyone else, including Him, also, on the guy, the doctors—I just blamed everybody. Then you have to take all of these names and write them down on a piece of paper, and you give them to the Lord. And you ask Him to forgive you, and then you just have to choose to forgive. You have to start the forgiving process and then you work through how the Lord sees you and how He wants us to see ourselves. You have to accept His love and His forgiveness. It's just a process you walk through. Lots of Bible verses show the love of God and the forgiveness of God. How much He loves you and does not condemn you. Holding any unforgiveness is just a trap of the enemy, him trying to destroy your life.

Now that I've had the healing classes, I can deal with the situation better on the sidewalk. I can talk to a woman before and after pain. Before pain, you just want to die. You have major, major guilt. It's going to hit hard. A post-abortive woman is going to try to bury it. A lot of women turn to drugs, alcohol, or suicide because of the guilt. If a woman says, "It's not going to bother me," it is, because she has no idea of how she'll feel after. She thinks she does, but she doesn't. You don't see much hope, you don't accept God's love. Even though He loves you, you refuse to accept it, because you feel like you know what the Word says, but your guilt is so deep you refuse to accept what the Word says, that it applies to you, that He forgives you for what you've done; you accept it for everyone else but yourself.

After the healing class, I accepted it. I accept that He loves me, that He forgives me. And I know that He does. I think every woman needs to go through that and experience that, because if not, the guilt will remain. And the woman also has to learn to forgive herself, which is very hard to do. Because you can have self-hatred, but after healing class, you don't have self-hatred. You can be at peace with yourself and be at peace with God. I think it's a must for every woman in such a hard place. Because if not, she may self-destruct (maybe not knowingly) but she may put herself into situations that are unhealthy, because deep down inside that's what she feels she deserves—no better—she doesn't deserve to be happy, or to be loved.

After healing class you feel you're worthy to receive the love of the Father, and the memorial class gives you total peace. The memorial class is where you name your baby. You get a death certificate, and you are accepting the fact that your baby is in the Father's arms, and that your child loves you and is waiting on you in heaven, and you get to say goodbye. It gives you closure. Like burying somebody, it gives you closure, which means a lot. You've acknowledged a life, a death, and you have closure. By the end, when you're going through the memorial, you've already accepted the forgiveness and love of the Father, so it's a beautiful thing, a healing ending. You light a candle in the memory of your child, and you have a rose, which symbolizes your baby, to put in a basket. They ask if you knew the sex of your child, and ask if you want to put the name on it. He put on my heart that it was a boy; I hadn't thought of a name yet, and when they asked me, Joshua Lee popped into my head. That closure is important because you get to say good-bye, but you know it's not the end, because they teach you that. The difference in the way I see myself today after having the class, and even the pain I still have, is that today I know that I am forgiven and I am loved.

Janet holding seven, eight, nine, and ten-week fetal models

From someone who knows, you've got to have compassion towards every abortion-minded woman that comes to an abortion clinic because you don't know her story, you don't know what brings her. It's got to be something devastating that actually brings her to that point. We can't be judgmental. It's something that I have to pray about sometimes, to ask the Lord to keep me focused on not getting judgmental, especially if I'm talking to a woman. The pain for me is there, but I just talk through the pain. The pain is not gone, and I ask Him to help me minister to her from that place. I can talk about it most of the time without breaking down. Sometimes I have to walk off and bawl for a minute. If you have a judgmental attitude toward that woman, she's going to immediately shut you down and run to have that abortion. That's going to be the icing on the cake for her, thinking that, "nobody cares," or, "I'm alone." It's going to push her there. It's the compassion and truth that is going to help open her eyes. To have the best outcome, we have to share the truth of God with love. We speak to the women through love, so they can see the love of the Lord with us being there, talking to them. Because most of them are going to feel abandoned—who knows what all they feel, but it's tragic, whatever brought them there, and there are underlying issues that nobody sees. It's life events that lead up to this point in time for her. She might have been raised in abuse, like myself, and that's all she ever knew. I know that if we condemn that woman, that baby's got no hope. Because immediately her heart, if it had any softness in it at all, is going to go cold and ice over. We need to let people know that Jesus loves them and that He loves their baby and there's always hope, even when they think there's no hope. We can give them information and show them different ways, give them resources—we've just got to let them know that we care. No matter how horrible they may be towards us, we still have to show them love.

About Miscarriage

At that 2019 March for Life, I also met Caitlin Jane, a talented singer/songwriter, at her booth, which was advertising her newest pro-life song entitled, "Unborn."[48] We took a selfie and I asked, "I know you've never met me before, but I'm a worship dancer and I feel led to ask you if I can dance to your song next month." She sweetly answered, "Yes, that would be great; make sure you send me the link to the performance so I can watch it." I thought that was amazing for her to tell me yes, even though she'd never met me before or even seen me dance!

She had written very compelling song lyrics, and when I heard them, I knew this was the song I was meant to use. I had one month until a televised interview, during which I would also perform, and

I choreographed and then practiced the dance quite a few times. The words really touched me, on so many levels. Obviously, I was talking to women all the time outside the abortion clinic about keeping their babies, and I was thrilled that some had chosen life, but devastated when others did not. Then, there was my personal story. Even though my mom had not consented when I was conceived, after I was born she ended up doing everything she could to keep me alive; in the end, she chose to pursue life for me. Still, it bothered me that I was not conceived in mutual love, and that she wasn't in love with me when she found out she was pregnant with me. My story is touching in that she finally did love me after I was born dead, but knowing the part before that hurt.

I struggled with overpowering emotions, often with tears streaming down my face as I rehearsed the dance. I cannot tell you how many tears I shed practicing this dance, and it even brings me to fresh tears now, when I watch the video three years later. I had to listen to it over and over to desensitize myself so I wouldn't be bawling while performing to it on live television. Believe it or not, there's yet one more reason it greatly affected me, and I've never before spoken of it publicly, until now.

It was mid-September of 2005, a month before our firstborn, Bryson, would turn two. We had all gone on a long weekend trip to the beach to celebrate our 12th anniversary. I had had an inkling that I was newly pregnant, noticing certain signs from my previous pregnancy recurring, and I was very excited about it. When we were at the steamy, warm beach I decided I definitely was. But the second day of our long weekend, to my horror, I discovered that I started discharging a lot of blood all at once. I went to a toilet and cried as I saw bloody clumps flushed away, realizing something was very wrong. I thought to myself, *I'm no longer pregnant.* That was confirmed the next day, when my body no longer had those same pregnancy signs; I was completely back to normal, pre-pregnancy state, and it was devastating.

At the time, I struggled with the questions of, "Why did this happen to me? What did I do wrong? Why didn't that little group of cells keep developing for nine months like my first healthy child?" I already had an almost two-year-old son, and I was extremely thankful for him; yet still, I wanted a little girl so badly and I wondered, *Will I ever be able to have another? Will this happen over and over? What can I do differently so that I don't miscarry again?* I had already told Robert I thought I was pregnant, and did not enjoy telling him, "Something went wrong, and I lost it." He was sad to hear it, but remained very supportive and encouraging.

I only ever mentioned it to my chiropractor, who said it happened, "Because things weren't right, that's why. Thank God for that self-correcting mechanism." He encouraged me to keep trying to have another child, and not worry about it anymore. So, thankfully, a few months later, we conceived again and I had another full-term pregnancy (Sydney). She actually stayed happily inside even nine days past the due date! After successfully delivering her, I basically shelved the whole miscarriage into the back of my mind without ever realizing I needed to go through any type of healing process; I didn't tell anyone else about it at the time.

After all, I was only in the first month of my pregnancy, and back then that would have been too early to take a pregnancy test; no one but my husband knew about it. I had friends who had had multiple miscarriages and/or miscarriages way into the second trimester. I knew they grieved a lot, but I had no idea that I might also need to go through a grieving process. I felt that I wasn't far enough along to have a right to grieve. But repressed emotions you shelve have a way of coming back up, and that's what eventually ended up happening to me.

When I became so involved in the pro-life movement, I began to think more about life starting at conception. That understanding affected me, because I came to realize that a unique being, with its own DNA, had been alive, forming inside of me. It didn't matter if it was three weeks old or three months old, the baby's death was a true loss, and I finally began a grieving process. I didn't really know what to do, though, so first I prayed and asked God if it was a boy or girl. I felt strongly that it was a boy. I knew that in abortion grieving classes, one of the main healing activities was to name your lost child, so that was my next step.

Robert and I were taking a trip to North Carolina for my birthday weekend in November 2018, and I brought up the subject, voicing all of those thoughts. I added, "That miscarriage was actually a life lost, and our child has gone back to God now. I prayed about it and feel that it was a boy, and I think we should give our child a name."

Robert was quiet for a while, shedding a couple of tears while thinking about a lost son he would not know here on earth. After some time, he said, "I think I'd like to name him John."

I said, "Why John? That's such a generic name."

He replied, "I like the name John because that's the disciple that Jesus loved."

"Well, that sounds like a great name to me," I responded, touched by his reasoning.

Unbeknownst to Robert, I kept thinking more over the coming months about giving our son a middle name. I decided that I really liked the name Daniel, because I so admire the Biblical character who stood, against all odds, for doing the right thing to honor God. The subject hadn't come up again, and I hadn't mentioned it to him or anyone else, for that matter. But God had listened.

In early 2019, my church held a series of classes, and one evening we were given specific tasks to listen to the Holy Spirit. My partner (who was no more than an acquaintance) was tasked with telling me a Biblical name that had great importance to me. I was quite astonished when she told me, "Daniel." That confirmed to me that yes, God had heard that I named my son John Daniel and was taking heavenly care of him.

I decided that yes, I should actually investigate grief classes to heal over the miscarriage. I did not find a class right away that worked out, but I was able to attend grief meetings at my church that year. The ironic thing was that I ended up realizing that I was also grieving over my father's death and over missing my foster children, and I was focused on those events during those meetings. I never was quite able to bring up the miscarriage; I just don't believe the timing was right.

I did, however, receive more counseling from Gene Wagstaff to help me with feelings of forgiveness towards myself, if I had done anything at all to cause the miscarriage. I did also search for local miscarriage grieving classes at the time, but nothing fit with my schedule.

God has perfect timing, and in early 2021 I was able to finally connect with a grief counselor at a local pregnancy resource center. She had some great points, and I'd like to share a couple of them, because they were so healing for me.

Some who have miscarriage might think they did something wrong or wonder what if they had done something differently, like they had some control over the situation. This is where I fell — into the category thinking I had done something wrong. I knew I had said, "I want a girl, not another boy next time," or, "There's no way I could handle two boys." I was beating myself up over the "what if's." Like, "What if I hadn't said that?" or, "What if I had been excited at the prospect of another baby, even if it were a boy?" That inward thinking left no room for the sovereign God to be in control. Satan loves to get us in a cycle of looking inwardly, where there's no hope. We must look at the eternal truth of who God is. I knew all this, but I hadn't applied it to my situation. Going forward, I can choose to keep looking back, but I'll be miserable if I stay there. 2 Corinthians 4:17-18 (NLT): "For our present troubles are small and won't last very long. Yet they produce for us a glory that vastly outweighs them and will last forever! So we don't look at the troubles we can see now; rather, we fix our gaze on things that cannot be seen. For the things we see now will soon be gone, but the things we cannot see will last forever."

The counselor explained something to me that I already knew — He's the one in full control. Psalms 139:16, which I have read so many times, actually tells us that He knows how many days each of us has. We all have an appointed amount of time to live. In Hebrews 9:27 He says we are destined to die — He makes the decision when, not us, and that death is precious to Him (Psalm 116:15). Although I remember so well that day which was heartbreak for me, it was a perfect day for my child, who beheld the face of God. God knew the days of John Daniel's existence here, and his death wasn't my doing. Even though I had been blaming myself, his days were actually appointed before his conception. That was his day to die, and there was nothing I could do to change it. I don't know why, but that was his appointed day to die and he is completely free. I'll never know why until I get to heaven, but I can trust Him. He's a good God, who is still sovereignly in control, regardless of my thoughts.

Another thing that had bothered me, though, was the fact that I wasn't very far along when I had the miscarriage—other women I knew were so much farther along in their pregnancies—did I really deserve to grieve when they had carried a child longer? And I had gone on to have another child after the miscarriage, whereas other women remained barren. I was almost embarrassed to even mention my grief since theirs must be so much worse. Well, she had an answer for that as well.

Our different hardships bind us together. We who have suffered loss are globally united, speaking the same painful language of loss. It doesn't matter that the loss is different, because the emotion of pain is universal, and it gives me an awareness to understand others. I can relate to and minister to them in their own grief. Satan desperately wants to isolate us, keeping us apart instead of helping others through their loss; God, however, uses us through our own experiences to bring hope to others.

In April 2021, that PRC hosted a memorial service for the parents who had gone through their miscarriage grief counseling classes. Robert and I were able to attend this special event, which honored six children, including our son, whose lives had ended even before taking their first breath. There were songs and scriptures, prayers and kind words. Each mother was given a beautiful white rose to place carefully in a basket, which symbolized putting our child in the hands of God. That was a sweet gesture, but my breath caught when I approached the candle we were to light to represent the life given by God. I hadn't realized that there would be a name place card with "John Daniel" at its base. My hand shook and Robert helped to steady it as we lit the candle together. During another part of the ceremony, I was caught off-guard at my deep emotions welling up when a presenter spoke the names of the unborn babies, and then the meanings of those names. "John" means "God is gracious," and "Daniel" means "God is my judge." Each parent was given a hand-crafted wooden box personalized with the baby's name on the lid. We were also given a certificate of life, to acknowledge that he was expected to be born, and that he went to be with Jesus before birth. It was a truly beautiful and thoughtful event that we greatly appreciated and will both cherish until we eventually see John Daniel in heaven.

John Daniel's memorial box

About Rape

When you use rape, incest, disability, poverty, or foster care as the reason abortion is necessary, you are telling millions of people who were conceived in, or have overcome these circumstances, that their life is not valuable. Our worth as humans isn't conditional, it is inherent.

—*Lila Rose, Live Action*[49]

What leads to the conception of a child doesn't negate the worth of the child.

—*Ryan Bomberger*[50]

Thanks to a friendly donor, my teenage daughter was able to come along with me to Washington, D.C. for the 2020 March for Life; this happened to be the first time ever a President of the United States had spoken live at the March. This time we went on a bus with a Protestant ministry group from Columbia, S.C., called A Moment of Hope.[51] They do amazing work outside of their abortion clinic, including supporting the mothers' needs during and after their pregnancies.

The previous year, I had visited a booth called "Save the One," which opened my eyes to the 1% who are aborted because their mothers were victims of rape. Like many others, I had thought that abortion wasn't okay, but I could understand why a woman who had been raped might consider it. The leader herself was saved from abortion and all of the other stories were powerful as well. That's when my eyes were opened to the idea that those children also deserve to live. Their website says, "Justice demands that only perpetrators pay for their crimes. We must not punish innocent children for someone else's crime. Rape and abortion are wrong for the same reason; they are both violent acts of aggression against another person. If you really care about rape victims, you should want to protect them from the rapist, and from the abortion, and NOT the baby. A baby is not the worst thing which can happen to a rape victim—an abortion is."[52] So actually, when a woman becomes a victim of rape and then murders her child, she has gone from being victim to perpetrator herself, and two wrongs don't make a right—instead, her grief is compounded.

My friend Kathy recently told me her own story as a victim of rape and abortion:

Decades ago, I was nearing the end of my freshman year of college when the unthinkable happened. I went to a party at an off-campus house and began searching upstairs for my boyfriend, who was asleep after a double shift. But before I found him, his friend came out of a room, threw me down a flight of stairs, and raped me. I packed up my things and left college within 72 hours. When I told my dad what had happened, he said, "Don't worry, you'll be fine." I started working at a hospital and discovered I was pregnant. I was even on the pill; it just doesn't always work like it should.

The hospital doctor told me there was a plan for people who wanted white children—I could have the baby and they would pay me. I didn't want to have anything to do with that because it sounded really weird and shady to me. Instead, I went to Chicago to an abortion clinic in 1972. At that point in time, people just told me, "Go have the abortion." There was no knowledge of the ramification of what you were actually doing to the child. I just wanted to take care of me, and looking back, it was for the wrong reasons; there was no guidance, no one telling me there were options. I was mortified and angered through the rape, and I thought I'd have anger towards the baby. At that point in my life I didn't have a great support system. Whether church, family, friends, whoever—support is critical

When I went for the abortion, I knew I was 16 weeks, but they didn't do an ultrasound back then. It was a cold atmosphere, with unfeeling people ordering, "Get in this chair...get in the stirrups... Spread your legs and we'll vacuum you... Here's medicine to make your pain go away." I felt like I was in an assembly line with everyone staring, all knowing they were there for the same reason. It was really frightening as hell. There was no counselor, you just gave your money and that was it. Not hearing, "What's best for you?" but a way for them to get money. You leave, and you have this loss of, "Oh my god, why did I let these people convince me this was the best way to go?"

I would tell people who are pregnant that the guilt will come. You can't ignore it; your body with all the hormones will get in touch with you. I would also say that there are so many people out there that would love to adopt a child that can't, and there are so many ways today that people can raise children as single parents and get help. I think the biggest stigma was if you weren't married and you were pregnant, in the 70s you were a whore, "How could you do this? You're disgusting." When I see newborns, I look at them in a whole different aspect than I did before. When you're young, if you don't have the right person to turn to, it's hard to make the right decisions. I was blessed to still have three children, but you never know. You may not be able to have children, no matter what they tell you. I think what Shiela is doing is valuable because she's giving them the option to hear what no one else may be telling them. I wish I'd made a different decision. I would not make the same decision now. All you have to do is have a child and look in their eyes and know you couldn't do anything else. I totally regret what I did, and every year I think about how old my child would have been, had I chosen differently.

About Adoption

"Together strong: life unites!" was the theme of the 2021 March for Life. I love the theme, because it is so true that people from all different backgrounds, religions, and races can all agree to unite on the sanctity of life. Very sadly, the march was mostly virtual, and only a very few people actually were allowed to march in person in Washington, D.C., due to the pandemic status. I did join others outside my local Greenville clinic that day, holding my "Abortion Hurts Women" sign. Although they left me alone that day, two counter-protestors were there with their electronic bullhorns, blaring sirens and bagpipe music, placing them right up to pro-lifers' ears, and pushing other sidewalk counselors out of the way when they tried to approach cars. Eventually, their antics that day led to one being arrested, and thankfully their activities interacting with us have slowed down overall since then.

This was the day I also met my new friend Amy, whose birth mother had been raped, became pregnant, and then chose adoption for her child:

My parents had adopted me when I was three months old; I can never remember not knowing that I was adopted. Growing up, I always felt special because I knew my wonderful parents had chosen me! At age 43, I received a letter from my birthmother, Sylvia. I learned that she had grown up in England during World War II. She chose to come to the United States in 1953 to live with an aunt and uncle. She felt there were more opportunities for jobs in the United States than in England; but after finding work, she had been "taken advantage of," and then had to go away to give birth to me. She was very happy to know that I had good parents and a happy life. She never had any other children. I learned that before releasing me to the adoption home she had named me Hope, and had a baby dedication ceremony praying for the parents I would be given. She was a Christian who loved the Lord and was active in a church.

We eventually met, and I am so thankful that God led her to me more than 40 years after she chose an adoption plan for me. Sylvia had no family in this country. I was her only child, and now she had a daughter and granddaughter. I tell people that I am so lucky to have been the only daughter to three mothers—my mother, my mother-in-law, and Sylvia. Don't let anybody ever tell you abortion is okay. I am here to tell you that every life is precious and important to our Lord.

About Abortion Pill Reversal

At a local pro-life rally in the spring of 2021, we had a doctor speak to us and explain how the abortion pill and the reversal process both work:

Progesterone (from German "pro-gestation") is very important in pregnancy to do the following: 1) it causes maturation of the lining of the uterus even before fertilization, 2) it keeps the placenta attached to the wall of the uterus so there's good nutrition flowing, 3) it relaxes the muscle of the uterus so there are no premature contractions, 4) it keeps the cervix tightly closed, and 5) it causes the breast cells to develop at just the right time to produce milk three days after delivery.

Mifepristone (taken day one of a chemical abortion) blocks the progesterone, which causes separation of the placenta from the wall of the uterus so that the baby no longer gets nutrition. The uterus softens, opens, and twitches as it begins to contract. This is an effective drug for ending a pregnancy, but isn't sufficient to expel the pre-born baby; therefore, misoprostol (Cytotec) pills are taken 24-48 hours later to cause strong uterine contractions, which should completely expel the remains of the pre-born baby.[53]

There is currently a progesterone-rich protocol for women who have already taken mifepristone on day one and then regretted their decision afterwards. This protocol, developed by Dr. George Delgado back in 2012, has a 64-68% success rate, with no increased rate of birth defects or early births. Statistics show that over 2,000 lives have been saved thanks to the abortion pill reversal protocol. Thankfully anywhere in the U.S., when a woman who has taken the mifepristone has regrets, the hotline is able to connect her with a provider who has been trained to administer this protocol to save lives.[54]

Molly and her husband told us their story at the same pro-life event. They didn't think they could handle having a child at that time, so she took the abortion pill in another state. Within hours of taking the first abortion pill, Molly knew she had made a terrible mistake. "When we got home later that night, we both just broke down," said Molly's boyfriend Cole. "It was just devastating. We knew it was the wrong choice and we regretted it very much." Desperate to save the life of their child, Molly and Cole called the abortion clinic to ask whether there was any way to reverse the abortion pill. The employee laughed at them. Fortunately, Molly and Cole didn't give up. They found an Abortion Pill Reversal doctor, who saved their baby! This is the story Molly wants to share:

This cause is so important to me because it saved my life. I would never have the relationship that I have with God today if it weren't for this decision. He has provided for every single need. We all know that God does things to work for His will.

My biggest fear and my biggest motivation to get an abortion was that I did not trust in God. I felt as if I wouldn't have enough to provide for my baby. Today I know for sure that God is holding me in His hands through this process, in this experience called life. God has gone above and beyond anything that I could have ever even wished for.

My baby son is healthy, strong, and beautiful. I know now with all my heart that God WILL provide for you and your baby; He loves you and will never abandon you—all you have to do is trust in Him!

12

Final Thoughts

There is no circumstance, no matter how desperate, that
justifies the killing of an innocent, unborn human being.
                                    —*Robert E. Jackson, Jr., M.D.*[55]

Shiela writing:

I thank God he is sending more workers out into the field now. But back in February 2019, I was dejected, sitting alone on my car bumper temporarily waiting hopefully for someone to come join me. Unbeknownst to me at the time, there had been a communication error with my partner's substitute, and she was coming, just a little later than I normally start. Since I didn't have a partner, I didn't approach any cars. I was angry and decided to rant on social media about the lack of workers in this ministry:

> So I've been here since 8:30. My regular partner had another commitment this morning and lined up someone else to come but she didn't show up. That means that for my own safety, I do not approach cars that are going into or coming out of the abortion clinic. Yes I am praying, but by myself and watching and crying as more and more women go in. I'm not upset because the second lady didn't show up or the first lady had another commitment. I'm upset that so many people say they are against abortion but yet we can't even

get three people at a time outside of this clinic while it's open to pray together, so that at least one can approach cars and in that way, make a difference. Surely God is calling more people.

Thankfully, we now have many more trained sidewalk counselors from several different ministries coming to help out. People like Jack are mobilizing local churches to participate, and God is also calling other individuals to come out on their own.

Another major rant from me that same year was about how Hollywood has infiltrated our way of thinking on abortion; we need to be aware of what we are watching and filter it through God's truth:

"What's on your mind, Shiela?" this social media application asks me. It has no idea I'm ready for a major rant. Here goes:

Please beware—Hollywood is finding different methods of sending out a subversive message about parenting as it relates to abortion, and that there are instances where it's okay because of inconvenience. One of the characters in a prime-time show I watch has an adult-age daughter in college who has made up her mind to have the procedure done so she doesn't lose out on a scholarship abroad, and is attempting to guilt-trip her father into being there to support her by paying and taking her to the clinic. His conscience just won't let him do it, so he goes looking for advice at a church but instead runs into the janitor. He tells him he can't figure out whether to be a good father or a good person, and the janitor tells him being a parent is like being God, who never leaves us even when we do the wrong thing. Of course, the father then decides and tells his daughter that although he's against it and still wants her to change her mind, he's going to do whatever she needs, then he hugs her and the audience is meant to feel all warm and fuzzy.

Do you see what is blatantly wrong with this picture??? GOD DOESN'T PAY FOR HIS CHILD TO HAVE

THE PROCEDURE AND/OR TAKE HER TO HAVE IT DONE!!! He causes roadblocks and other problems to help stop it from happening. And He sends people like me, just in case someone wants to stop, talk, and find out if there's another option besides ending a life that God created.

I might have fallen for this mental trap in the past, but I've learned a lot on the subject in the past year. At the March for Life I saw the "Silent No More" marchers who have regrets. I heard their speeches, and many of them were from women regretting their abortions, but many speeches also were given by both men and women saying how they regretted being an accomplice to the act by taking their friend, daughter, wife, etc. to have the procedure done.

A friend I'm on the sidewalk with weekly has told me her sister's story also. Their mom was trying to be supportive of her daughter and took her, even though she was against the procedure. Her sister felt tremendous grief and guilt and had another baby to try to remove the pain. Then she tried to mask it with drugs. Nothing else helped, so she committed suicide and orphaned her toddler.

I hear stories like this all the time, folks. It doesn't turn out well unless and until God heals. I've also heard many testimonies that He can and does heal, which is amazing, and He is faithful, but the memory and regret of the child lost is always there. And please don't think I wouldn't love my child unconditionally and take care of her in every way possible after the fact, because I would most definitely. But I'd take air out of her car tires or anything else in my power to keep her from getting to that appointment to spare her from agony and regret.

If you don't agree with me, that's your right to free speech, just as this is my right, and hopefully we can amicably agree to disagree. Some things just need to be said. We have to stand up for what we believe, and we'll all be held accountable one day. I know I've helped save at least 14 babies, but I have to believe the number is much higher, and one day I'll find out. I pray for the 500 plus that have been lost just during the time when I've stood outside that fence in the last 14 months. I also love and offer non-judgmental support, healing information, and prayers for those women who come out of the clinic after losing a child. Please don't judge someone harshly if you find out they've lost a child to abortion, because usually they felt they had no other option. That's why I stand in the sun and cold, wind and rain, just in case they want to hear another option....

It's possible that throughout this book, you may not have agreed with me and/or with Dionne on our personal thoughts and beliefs. As you can easily see, Dionne and I are different in a variety of ways. We come from different parts of the country, have different skin color, and have a different family background. However, we're almost the same age, and we both have love for God, our country, and our families. And most importantly, for the purpose of this book, we are both united in the agreement that abortion isn't the best choice for women and pro-lifers will accomplish more if they have loving, non-judgmental attitudes.

I didn't know why I felt the Holy Spirit urging me to meet with Dionne, but I was just following His prompting when to reach out to contact her. I know it wasn't something I would have come up with on my own. I certainly didn't have any ulterior motive, no hidden agenda at all, because she already obviously knew my heart was that abortion didn't exist AND that she didn't work there. There wasn't anything more. I must admit that I was curious why the Holy Spirit was having me reach out, and also why in the world she responded positively. The whole thing was really just very strange to both of us, but God wanted me to show love towards her and get to know her. He loved her, even though she was working in a less than ideal situation.

I didn't brag about it; I kept it completely quiet from my pro-life friends. To the ones who stood with me, though, they could see we were very friendly with each other and commented on it often. I could have easily taken advantage of our friendship, but I respected her work position and didn't want to incriminate her in any way, or make her think I was just using her, because that certainly wasn't in my heart.

It's about meeting someone where they are and loving them regardless of their situation. Sure, I encouraged her to find work elsewhere, but I knew that was a decision between her and God. We've all made choices we regret and, hopefully, learned from the process. None of us deserve grace, but God has freely given it to us anyway. If He can show grace to me, a sinner, and can forgive me for all I do, how can I not forgive others?

Someone recently asked me if I think God places certain people to work in abortion clinics. I most certainly do not believe that, but I do believe He can still use them for His purpose, wittingly or not. In getting to know Dionne and her story, I believe that He has used her whenever possible to encourage women coming for abortions to choose life instead. I know for a fact that He wants to use her to impact women who read this book to realize what a gift a new life is and to not take it for granted.

God has called Dionne to use her life for something more than working in an abortion clinic. I know that's not her true destiny as a child of God and that He's called her to a higher purpose. It's her job to follow in the path He's set out for her to be obedient, as He leads. I do also know that God has called her to expose the truth that abortion is not the best choice for women, and she will be blessed for following in that calling. I'm very excited to see where He leads her next as she leaves the clinic work behind her forever.

What Should Christians Do for the Battle?

As warriors for the Lord, for the unborn,...because we're in a battle...we have to stay pure in the eyes of God to be able to be His voice to those...the only way to win this battle, I believe,...is through transforming hearts with love.

— *Sr. Deirdre "DeDe" Byrne, POSC*[56]

For everyone has sinned; we all fall short of God's glorious standard.

Romans 3:23 (NLT)

Discerning sin isn't the problem; it's what we do with it that counts. If love isn't present, our discernment can lead us into judgment. Love pulls people to us like a magnet, but judgment repels. Judgment and love cannot co-exist. We cannot have true influence over anyone or anything we don't love.

—David Fritch[57]

A new command I give you: Love one another. As I have loved you, so you must love one another. By this everyone will know that you are my disciples, if you love one another.

John 13:34-5 (NIV)

I've seen a lot of literature since I've been a pro-life advocate, and the one piece that hit me the hardest explained how European Christians behaved during their worship services. They knew that trainloads of Jews crying out for help were passing behind their church building as they sang their hymns. Instead of taking any helpful action, all they did was sing a little louder to cover up the noise.[58] I have visited Dachau and was horrified by the scene of death camps which killed an estimated 11 million peoples of many different nationalities, including many Jews, during the Holocaust. It was so indescribably awful, as is over 62 million[59] in our country dying from abortion just since Roe v. Wade was passed. Christians need to speak up for mankind, for ourselves as citizens, born and unborn! If you're a Christian, you cannot be silent in this battle, or just "sing a little louder." When the Day of Judgement comes, do you want to be remembered for how loudly you sang, or what you did to save the unborn while the evil one was trying to extinguish them?

Pastors, don't close your eyes to this atrocity happening around you! Up to one third[60] of the women in your congregation may have had abortions; shepherd them with healing counseling. Preach that abortion is not in alignment with God's word so that it's not the first idea a pregnant woman resorts to. Encourage and strengthen the men in your congregation to stand up for women and their unborn children, providing for and protecting them. Teach youth they should not have premarital sex, and if they do, abortion is not an option that they should consider. Empower your congregation to step up and be a part of the solution, not the problem!

Come awake, O sleeping church, rise up O sleeper! Don't tell me you'd be embarrassed that someone would see you standing outside an abortion clinic, or you're worried someone might yell at you as they drive by. This is not a time for fear of man—stand up for what is right; women's lives are being ruined, and their children are dying.

> It is quite true that the way to live a godly life is not an easy matter. But the answer lies in Christ.
> 1 Timothy 3:16

Abortion was begun in evil hearts, and it has evil outcomes. With the evil rampant in this world, it does seem that some will choose to have abortions until the second coming of Christ. Until then, as Christians, we need to do everything we can to lovingly win hearts and minds through the love of God. I strongly believe that God in the Bible has ordained that sex should only be between a married man and woman. That is one way that unwanted pregnancies would be significantly reduced. The problem, though, is that when sex occurs outside of marriage and a woman gets pregnant, church is the last place she wants to be seen. She already feels she made a mistake and is often alone with no helpful male. She knows the church will not approve of her behavior and it's possible that she fears she might be shunned, so she calls the abortion clinic instead.

I've seen firsthand what abortion does to women, and it's not pretty. We need to support and love women and come alongside them so abortion does not need to be an option in our country. The issue of abortion is a spiritual battle that will only be won when we can change the hearts and minds of everyone, when we are only full of love and not judgment towards abortion-minded women and the abortion workers. Fellow Christians, we must be Jesus' hands and feet to the hurting, helping these women in trouble so they feel that the church is a loving environment that will help them in their time of need.

Churches need to recognize the need for ending abortion by providing help to pregnant mothers. Thankfully, there are nation-wide and local programs that that do a fantastic job of coming alongside a new mother in caring support, drawing her closer in friendship to Jesus through a loving church body. These programs not only help save a life, but can help with the salvation of the mother as well. There are great examples of how to support women, so churches need to partner with an organization that is already doing it well, and then let their congregation know how to help. My hope and prayer is that even more churches would join in these supportive programs. If we can mobilize the church body and change their way of thinking from shaming pregnant women to empowering them, we can all work towards ending abortion.

Laws are constantly changing, and another great way in South Carolina, or your state, to help effect a change for life is with your voting power. All over the United States, legislators are working to pass new laws that are friendlier to the unborn. Many believe that Roe v. Wade eventually will be overturned at the federal level—and I pray it does—, and then the issue of abortion will once again be determined at the state level. South Carolina has just passed a new Heartbeat bill in February of 2021. Although it's already tied up in litigation, it was passed to be an incremental step. This bill looks at the science, showing the mother that there is a heartbeat, often showing up by six weeks on the ultrasound. Many mothers choose life when they actually see the heartbeat and realize they are hosting a living human.

It would be wonderful to eradicate abortion completely here, but even this new law enforced could not be enough; abortions will still be legal here for nearly the first two months of the baby's gestation. Although it's a step in the right direction, abortion is still sin, and we as Christians can't just be content to let the matter drop.

Life begins at conception, so new legislation needs to be passed to protect it from that initial point. Sanctity of life is paramount, and a new personhood bill would ban ALL abortion. South Carolina does have staunch Christian legislators who introduced yet another bill on March 11, 2021, that goes a step further that would abolish all abortions in this state and also prosecute abortionists. May it pass into law, and may South Carolina be the first state in the union to be abortion-free!

The new human zygote that I discussed at the beginning of the book has a genetic composition that is absolutely unique to itself, different from any other human that has ever existed, including that of its mother, thus disproving the pro-choice claim that what is involved in abortion is merely "a woman and her body." It took two people to form that zygote, and the father also needs to be involved. Men need to stand up and take their place alongside their women to support them and their unborn AND born children! Men are meant to be the patriarch, the priest, the provider, and the protector of their families—I do believe they need to step up and have a say in what happens to their children's futures, but then follow through with fulfilling their God-given family roles.

I am virtually a newbie in this movement, standing on the faithful perseverance of those who have gone before me, and reaping the benefits of their labors. Pro-lifers in Greenville have been praying for over 30 years now that all of our abortion clinics would shut down. So far, there is only one left in the battle. Eventually, it will also close, whether because the abortionists decide to retire, or legislature is passed to abolish abortion in South Carolina, or because they have a change of heart that what they are doing is contrary to God's law.

> For God...is looking for those with changed hearts and minds.
>
> *Romans 2:29*

I ask you, after reading this book, how do we finally prevail and win? What attitudes do we need to have to change the hearts and minds of the unexpectedly pregnant parents in our region?

How should we treat abortion workers? Will anger, hate and unforgiveness work? Or should we approach with grace, love, and forgiveness? Look to the cross. How did God treat us for our sins? We've all sinned and fallen short of His glory, but He loved us so much that He sent His Son to die on the cross for our sins. He forgave us of all our sins, showing us His grace and mercy, and so we forgive others as well. God loves that mother who just lost a child to abortion, or that abortion worker just as much as He loves you or me. That's a tough pill for some to swallow, but it's the plain truth, like it or not.

> *Because of his deep love and concern for you, you should*
> *practice tenderhearted mercy and kindness to others.*
> *Colossians 3:12*

Obviously God hates abortion, but we want to help lead people to repentance, not push them farther away from their loving Father by being harsh. How will some of them even know what He's like unless they experience Him through encounters with us? Aren't we to be the light of the world? You may have a better argument, but is it going to save unborn lives? Is it more important for you to be self-righteous, or to be loving and win over hearts? Don't forget, we've all sinned and fallen short.

So, I say we should definitely pray for the end to abortion in not just our state, but our country as well. Also, vote for those who can write the laws into being. Get your church involved in supporting pregnant, needy women. Teach your teenagers abstinence until marriage and the horrors of how abortion hurts women AND men. Attend pro-life events near you. Volunteer at a pregnancy resource center. Donate financially into pro-life ministries. You get the picture: the list is endless. The trick in succeeding is praying into what God is calling you to do, and then do it well—do it faithfully and on a regular basis. Do what you can to make a positive change in others' hearts and minds about abortion. Yes pray, but also take loving action as God leads you to make a difference. Make connections in love.

Next, make it a priority to plan a visit with your friends and/or family outside an abortion clinic to pray. It's your legal right, and I personally believe, your moral obligation as a Christian, to go pray outside an abortion clinic. People can come up with all the excuses in the world as to why they can't go. It's true that people have different seasons in their lives, but ALL seasons should be pro-life in one way or another. If you work full-time, go for an hour on a weekend to pray. People that really want to go can find a way. I've seen the elderly with canes or even walkers who bring their chairs, people with little kids strapped into strollers or baby carriers, and people who work full-time come on a day off. I understand you may not have the time and/or resources to come out two mornings a week like I do, and certainly not everyone has a calling for sidewalk ministry, but surely you can find an hour once or twice a year? Even just to sit in your car and pray for those entering and exiting the premises? Imagine the show of solidarity if all the Christians around Greenville came to stand in support of the unborn just one hour a year—there would be a mob of people nonstop all day, every day!

When (not if) you go to an abortion clinic, pray first for a heart like Christ's, and approach the situation with love as a priority. Show empathy towards what the mother is feeling and going through. A pregnancy throws her mind and body for a loop anyway, even in the best of circumstances. She's probably scared, upset, and feels alone; don't barrage her with judgment and criticism. Now is the time to be Jesus to her and demonstrate His tender mercy, to lead her to the compassionate love of the Father, so she'll be convicted to choose life for her baby. Also, pray for the women who have lost children to abortion. They are coming out wounded, often feeling hopeless and depressed. They need our prayers and support so that they can receive the healing God provides and not choose the same mistake again.

Let me be very clear—I do not shame women who have had abortions. My desire to save babies isn't greater for any particular race, and the care and love I feel for the moms doesn't stop even if they make a choice that I don't agree with. I was called to minister to moms and they are still mothers after they've lost a child to abortion. I understand they feel they have no other alternatives. They have been lied to by societal norms that it was a good choice, the best choice they could make. But that's why I'm there—to offer them hope for healing and to feel God's love. I don't want anyone on my watch saying that no one was there when they entered the clinic, as a sign that they shouldn't do it. I'm the last person they'll speak with before they get inside that clinic, and I want to educate them about other alternatives, if they're only willing to listen.

Remember also to pray for the abortion clinic workers; they are likewise loved by God. I believe they often think they are doing a helpful service for women, although it has been shown in exposés that there can be nefarious happenings behind the scenes. Our greatest desire should be that they have a change of heart; again, that can happen better if we demonstrate love towards them rather than hate. Would Dionne and I have ever become friends if I had yelled at her on a regular basis? I think not.

God specifically prepared me for this calling. I now know that I would not be as powerful a force if I had not traveled the journey of my own difficult birth, and had such a powerful story to share with others who are making a life and death decision. But being called was a process of God working on my heart. It was a journey, beginning with being obedient to writing my first book, and then going through the difficulties of fostering. I feel that He tested my faithfulness on those two subjects first, before entrusting me to a ministry this important. Then, as I was sensitive to His calling, He led me into friendship with Dionne and our amazing journey together to inform people how abortion hurts women. This book is a testimony about what can happen when someone says yes when His voice is heard calling them into truth, and then boasts in what the Lord has done.

> As it says in the Scriptures, "If anyone is going to boast,
> let him boast only of what the Lord has done."
>
> 1 Corinthians 1:31

The publishing of this book in September 2021, marks my three-year anniversary of my personal ministering time outside the abortion clinic, which equals the following:

- Over 300 actual days/750 hours in ministry at "the sidewalk,"

- Over 700 times I gave out multiple pieces of literature and gifts,

- Over 125 times when women chose to not even enter the clinic,

- Over 35* times when women chose life, and praise God,

- One time an abortion worker became my friend.

(*At our clinic, we've heard reports of well over 100 women choosing life during that three-year time period, but I was only present for 35. However, we now know that quite a few more choose life on a regular basis—they just don't stop to tell us.)

Shiela, Janet and I were outside the [abortion] clinic a while back and we were talking about the people who worked at the clinic. Many of them are nice people. From time to time they stop, talk, and appear to be the type of people with whom you could build a friendship. I began to wonder why a person with a pleasant disposition would work in a clinic that does abortions. Shiela and Janet immediately called my attention to the possibility that these people thought that they were helping the clients of the clinic and recommended that we pray for the abortion clinic workers as much as we do for the clients at the clinic. They are correct, and I thank them for helping me to continue to grow as a Christian.

—Paul

Shiela is very personable and positive. She is confident and bold, but not pushy or judgmental. Her presence and smile convey faith and hope and love. Her life story, through her mother's struggle and through her own two children whom she loves so much, is directly relevant to those entering the abortion facility and struggling with abortion decisions. I can say that for most of us starting out, it definitely feels awkward, and it can be hard to guide the conversation with a perfect stranger, especially when the time may be limited by a car entering from behind, but Shiela picked it up quickly. Soon she was effectively sharing information with car occupants and gaining their trust. Because Shiela is so relational and Spirit-led, she can pick up on who they are and where they're at and meet them there, sometimes crying with them and sometimes laughing with them to lighten the mood, and always offering them real help for their needs and circumstances. She has seen many mothers choose life and has kept in touch with some, providing them on-going help and encouragement and watching their babies grow.

—Carrie

I have observed Shiela for over two years now, working directly with her out on the sidewalk. During this time I have observed Shiela approaching people going in and out of the abortion clinic, and from all walks of life, with a loving, compassionate, and non-judgmental approach. Her love for the unborn and for humanity in general is readily apparent for all to see who care to watch and learn from her.

Shiela has never met a stranger, and that loving, kindness-centered manifestation of the heart of Jesus even extends with Shiela to ministering to the abortion clinic workers. It takes a special kind of person to love those who strongly disagree with you. Abortion workers are not our enemy, but in certain situations they can be our adversaries. Since love conquers all, Shiela has been able to put that wisdom to good use by reaching out to the abortion clinic workers and doctors either by waving and smiling or offering help, advice and prayers for them.

Her approach has worked, especially with one worker in particular who always stops on her way into the clinic to share a few words with Shiela. Slowly but surely the war for people's hearts, minds and souls is being won. Perhaps one day very soon in Greenville, S.C., we will see an abortion worker quit and move to the side of saving lives rather than taking lives. We will have the Lord and His anointed to thank for that.

—Bob

What About You?

If you want to know what God wants you to do, ask Him, and He will gladly tell you. But when you ask Him, be sure that you really expect Him to tell you.

James 1:5-6

Dear brothers, what's the use of saying that you have faith and are Christians if you aren't proving it by helping others? Will that kind of faith save anyone?

James 2:14

What ministry has God prepared you for and is calling you to? What connections is God calling you to make? Do you hear Him clearly? Are you doing your part to further His kingdom here on earth?

Please remember, we need to see others from the viewpoint that God sees them, through His lens of love. He sent Jesus to die on the cross for the sins of all mankind, and He sees people differently than we do; He sees them in their true identity, as they are washed clean and forgiven, pure from the blood sacrifice of His Son. We must do all we can in love to bring others to Him, to true repentance, and to help them understand their ultimate destiny as His sons and daughters of the Most High King.

The End...

For Now

Unborn

—by Caitlin Jane[61]

I am unborn. I cannot speak when I am afraid,
You can feel a silent cry.
My eyes have not yet seen the colors of this world,
But what you do to me shows me death or life.

For your choice is all I have. Your voice my only chance.
Please keep me.

I am alive, my heart is beating.
Innocent life, small inside I hide. I need you all the time.
Someday I'll grow up,
Just because of you, who cared enough to love.

For your choice is all I have. Your voice my only chance.
Please keep me.

My life here is at your mercy, don't you see.
I am unborn, my entire life ahead of me. I am your baby.
The world awaits my cry and breath,
I long to be held in your arms Mommy.
God's depth of love for you is everlasting.
In the dark, or in the light, He'll never leave.

Though I may be little, unnoticed,
Please don't let me stay unnoticed for too long.
God makes no mistakes.
Both you and I are wonderfully, fearfully made.

For your choice is all I have.
Your voice my only chance. Please keep me.
Your choice is all I have.
Your voice my only chance. Please keep me.

Special Thanks

From Shiela:

To God my Sustainer who has led me on this special path, guiding me on every step of the journey.

To my husband Robert for his loving, staunch support of my pro-life ministry.

To my children, Bryson and Sydney, for being so very patient when mom was busy for months "working on the book."

From Dionne:

To God, the Life-Giver, I would not be here without you.

To my children, Demetria and Desmond, whom I love with all my heart.

From Both Authors:

To Anne Huff for generously allowing the quotes from her book.

To Michelle Calloway Bowden for designing a beautiful book cover.

To Valerie Baronkin for patiently taking cover photos until Shiela was satisfied with the final result.

To Peggy Scolaro and others (you know who you are!) for lending valuable editorial expertise.

To all the reviewers and proofreaders for taking your time and effort to help us complete this project; we greatly appreciate you.

Dionne's Foster Puppy

Afterword

Dionne writing:

The nine months for this project to come to completion have been a little scary and a little exciting—it's like having a baby. During this time period I've had a lot of crazy things going on in my life. There have been many ups and downs. Over the course of four months, three close family members passed away, which saddened me greatly and therefore was very distracting, pulling my attention away from the book.

As a belated birthday present to myself early this spring, I invested in a newer car, which lightened my spirits. Within two weeks, however, I was rear-ended, but it was minimal damage, mostly cosmetic.

Not long after that, on my daughter's birthday, I got shot in the backside while I was sleeping in my bed. Thankfully, it was relatively painless and I did not suffer any long-term health issues. Even though I had been there for over a decade and it was a relatively peaceful street, I decided it was time for a change of neighborhoods and moved farther away from downtown Greenville.

I tried fostering a puppy named Dallas for a few weeks, but then I realized dogs are just too much work and I'll stick with my cat. Dallas was adorable though, and she brought me some joy; she just didn't grow on me.

And lastly, I have updated my resume and am currently looking for a career change. I know Father will open a door for me. I'm excited to step into the next chapter of the story He has written over my life.

> *"For I know the plans I have for you," declares the Lord,*
> *"plans to prosper you and not to harm you, plans to give*
> *you hope and a future."*
>
> *Jeremiah 29:11 (NIV)*

SWITCH's mission is to end human trafficking and sexual exploitation in the Upstate of South Carolina. Human trafficking is a deep-rooted issue and often touches many other issues, including abortion. Several women we have worked with over the years have been forced to have abortions by their traffickers. At the same time, many women may have felt abortion was their only option in some excruciating circumstances. We have often heard how the wounds from either run incredibly deep and potentially impact them for years. We do not pass judgment on the women in their choices or lack thereof. We hope to walk with them as they find healing from the many traumas related to trafficking, exploitation, and abortion.

At SWITCH, we believe in a Savior who can eradicate trafficking, exploitation, and abortion. We believe that He will do it. In the meantime, we are working to be His "hands and feet" to those who have experienced them and find healing as needed.

www.SwitchSC.org

(Net proceeds from sales of this book will be donated to SWITCH.)

Resources to Learn More About:

To see all the main informative brochures our pro-life group hands out locally, visit: www.love4you.life.

TO FIND CRISIS PREGNANCY HELP NEAR YOU

www.OptionLine.org

THE ABORTION PILL (RU-486)

Informative video: https://www.lifeissues.org/a-closer-look-at-the-chemical-abortion-pill

ABORTION PILL REVERSAL

If you have taken the abortion pill (RU-486), please contact the abortion pill reversal hotline right away at 1-877-558-0333. www.abortionpillreversal.com

ADOPTION

If you are pregnant and considering abortion, please instead consider making an adoption plan! Call Quiver Full Adoptions in the Greenville, S.C. area at (864) 334-8593. www.quiverfulladoptions.com

POST-ABORTIVE SUPPORT

If you are looking for immediate emotional support after an abortion, you can call OptionLine at 1-800-712-4357. They have a chat available online at: https://optionline.org/after-abortion-support/

Have you lost a child to abortion or aided someone in the process of abortion and you want to speak out about the negative impact it had on your life? Consider reaching out to the Silent No More Awareness campaign to share your story. www.silentnomoreawareness.org

RAPE

Save the 1: https://www.savethe1.com/

Radiance Foundation: https://www.theradiancefoundation.org/

ABUSED OR HOMELESS

Safe Harbor (Greenville) 1-800-291-2139: https://www.safeharborsc.org/

National free helplines, directories, and support organizations for assistance with homelessness, domestic violence, or mental health issues: https://www.samhsa.gov/homelessness-programs-resources/grant-programs-services/path-program/immediate-assistance

HUMAN TRAFFICKING

If you or someone you know is being sex trafficked, call 1-888-373-7888 or text "Help" to 233733.

SWITCH

Founded in 2012, SWITCH is a grassroots organization leading a movement to end human sex trafficking and sexual exploitation in the Upstate of South Carolina. www.switchsc.org

LEGISLATIVE

South Carolina Citizens for Life, Inc., is a non-profit, single issue, right-to-life organization devoted to restoring legal protection to the unborn and to protecting innocent human life by eliminating abortion, infanticide, and euthanasia from our society. https://www.sclife.org/

Contact the Authors:

www.ConnectionAtTheFence.com

ENDNOTES:

[1] https://www.merriam-webster.com/dictionary/abortion

[2] Evelyn's 90th birthday celebration May 2021 in Oregon.

[3] https://kingdomwinds.com/advocating-pro-life-on-a-sidewalk/

[4] According to email from SCDHEC Interim Director of Biostatistics, Jun Tang, PhD, MS, South Carolina DHEC reports that at Greenville's clinic in 2019 there were 2,133 abortions, and in 2020 there was a slight increase to 2,274 abortions.

[5] https://greenvillefor.life/ Abortion counter.

[6] https://www.tigernet.com/update/Death-Valley-ranked-No-1-stadium-in-CFB-29311

[7] Amos 1:13, Hosea 14:1

[8] Exodus 21:22-25

[9] Leviticus 20:2

[10] Exodus 1:15

[11] Matthew 2:16

[12] https://www.youtube.com/watch?v=j7wDiCll024&ab_channel=TechInsiderTechInsider

[13] https://www.history.com/topics/womens-rights/roe-v-wade

[14] https://supreme.justia.com/cases/federal/us/410/179/

[15] https://www.ortl.org/the-facts/oregons-history/

[16] https://www.guttmacher.org/state-policy/explore/overview-abortion-laws

[17] Anne Huff, *The Awakening, The Pro-Life Movement in South Carolina, Learning from the Past to Shape the Future.*, (Self-Published, 2010), 2.

[18] Ibid., 41.

[19] Ibid., 5-6.

[20] Ibid., 7-8.

[21] Ibid., 11.

[22] Ibid., 17, 28.

[23] Ibid., 6-7, 11, 33.

[24] Ibid., 123.

[25] Ibid., 7.

[26] https://greenvillefor.life/

[27] https://www.amazon.com/Mrs-Shiela-Honbeck-Miller/e/B00J2IZ76S/ref=dp_byline_cont_pop_book_1

[28] https://www.facebook.com/122338921302871/videos/465113930358700

[29] https://youtu.be/qS0HLwVj3uQ

[30] https://www.webmd.com/women/guide/d-and-c-dilation-and-curettage

[31] Partial-birth abortion was banned in November 2003 by George Bush but has never come into effect. https://www.ncbi.nlm.nih.gov/pmc/articles/PMC1388155/#:~:text=The%20case%20might%20lead%20to,2003%3B327%3A1009

[32] Scroll down to view brochure at: www.love4you.life

[33] https://www.mayoclinic.org/tests-procedures/medical-abortion/about/pac-20394687

[34] https://lovelife.org/america/

[35] Scroll down to view brochure at: www.love4you.life

[36] (Students for Life of America, Facebook video of Alveda King, Entitled, "Why African Americans Should Care About Abortion.") https://m.facebook.com/story.php?story_fbid=161622655279326&id=79125112926

[37] http://www.wogcounseling.org/

[38] https://www.intouchfertility.com/blog/2018/1/2/example-post-5

[39] https://www.guttmacher.org/news-release/2018/about-half-us-abortion-patients-report-using-contraception-month-they-became

[40] https://www.hli.org/resources/naprotechnology/

[41] www.love4you.life

[42] https://naturalwomanhood.org/
https://www.factsaboutfertility.org/
https://onemoresoul.com/

[43] Theresa Burke, Ph.D. with David C. Reardon, Ph.D., *Forbidden Grief: The Unspoken Pain of Abortion*, (Springfield, Illinois: Acorn Books, 2002), 46.

[44] Ibid.

[45] Ibid.

[46] Ibid., 47.

[47] Scroll down to view brochure at: www.love4you.life

[48] https://www.caitlinjanetunes.com/

[49] https://www.liveaction.org/

[50] https://www.theradiancefoundation.org/

[51] https://amoh.org/

[52] https://www.savethe1.com/

[53] https://vimeo.com/500525113/099d68c2eb

[54]
https://www.youtube.com/watch?v=RNehqlRftlc&t=2s&ab_channel=LiveAction

[55] Robert E. Jackson, Jr., M.D., *The Family Doctor Speaks: The Truth About Life*, (Self-Published, 2017), 43.

[56] Taken from speech at a pro-life event on Nov. 1, 2020.

[57] David Fritch, *Enthroned*, (Self-Published for Kindle, 2017), Chapter 12.

[58] https://kingdomworks.com/films/sing-a-little-louder/

[59] https://www.foxnews.com/politics/abortions-since-roe-v-wade

[60] https://www.focusonthefamily.com/pro-life/survey-women-go-silently-from-church-to-abortion-clinic/ 2015 study shows more than 4 in 10 women were churchgoers when they had their abortion.

[61]
https://www.youtube.com/watch?v=oleNbSmZptc&t=3s&ab_channel=GlenElliott

Made in the USA
Columbia, SC
20 September 2021

45239567R00122